LGBTQ+ MENTAL HEALTH AND ADVOCACY GUIDE

Practical Strategies, Inspiring Stories, and Guided Support to Overcome Challenges and Build Inclusive Lives

ALEX HARPER

Contents

Introduction

Every day, members of the LGBTQ+ community face unique mental health challenges and systemic barriers that seek to undermine their pursuit of well-being and equality. The urgency to address these issues is more than just necessary – it's critical for fostering a society that champions inclusivity and resilience. This book results from my commitment to advocating for mental health support and inclusive practices within the LGBTQ+ community. I aim to empower you with knowledge, inspire you with stories of courage, and equip you with the tools to advocate for yourself and others.

The 'LGBTQ+ Mental Health and Advocacy Guide' is crafted to serve a broad audience. Whether you are an LGBTQ+ individual encountering the nuances of your mental health journey, a therapist aiming to provide better support, a healthcare provider, an educator, or an ally seeking effective ways to participate in advocacy, you will find valuable insights and guidance here. Each chapter intertwines personal narratives with strategic advice, creating a comprehensive guide that addresses the mental, emotional, and social challenges faced by the LGBTQ+ community.

One particularly transformative moment for me was witnessing a close friend, after years of internal struggle and external discrimination, find a supportive community that embraced her whole identity. This experience underscored the profound impact that understanding, acceptance, and advocacy can have on individuals and the community. These stories of transformation and the lessons they carry are threaded throughout this book.

The landscape of LGBTQ+ rights and mental health is ever-changing, and thus, this book is not just a one-time read but a resource to be revisited as you continue to learn and grow. You should approach these pages with an open heart and mind, ready to absorb the personal stories and engage with shared strategies.

Let us move forward together with hope and solidarity, committed to building a world where every member of the LGBTQ+ community not only survives but thrives. Your journey through the *'LGBTQ+ Mental Health and Advocacy Guide'* is a step toward that world—a world where collective understanding and action bring about profound, positive change.

ONE

Understanding LGBTQ+ Identities and Experiences

Have you ever felt like the world around you was designed with a manual you never received? For many within the LGBTQ+ community, this feeling is a common thread that connects many of our stories. This chapter allows us to explore and validate our diverse identities and experiences. It's about giving you the words and understanding to articulate who you are, and equally important, it's about challenging the widespread misconceptions that often influence the perception of LGBTQ+ lives. Here, you'll find not just definitions but stories, context, and the affirmation that your identity is valid—and that you're not alone in this.

Defining Gender and Sexuality Spectrum: Beyond Binary Norms

In our society, gender and sexuality are often presented as binary: male or female, straight or gay. However, the reality is much more colorful. **Gender identity** refers to one's internal understanding of gender, which may or may not correspond with the sex assigned at birth. **Gender expression** involves how an individual presents their gender externally through clothing, behavior, hairstyle, voice, and more. **Sexual orientation** is about who you are attracted to, whether it be emotionally, romantically, or physically, and it is independent of gender identity.

Understanding gender and sexuality as spectrums means recognizing that these elements of identity exist in a wide range of possibilities, not confined to traditional or binary options. For instance, someone might identify as nonbinary, which means their gender identity does not fit neatly into the categories of 'man' or 'woman.' Another might describe their sexual orientation as pansexual, reflecting an attraction to people of all gender identities.

Let's break down some terms you might encounter:

- **Bisexual**: Attracted to more than one gender.
- **Pansexual**: Attracted to people regardless of gender.
- **Genderqueer**: A gender identity that is not exclusively male or female and may exist outside these binary options.
- **Asexual**: Experiencing little to no sexual attraction to others, irrespective of gender (though romantic attraction might still exist).

Through real-life examples, consider Randy, a pansexual individual who finds themselves attracted to people of various gender identities. Their story reflects the fluidity of attraction, challenging the common misconception that people must have a preference for either the opposite sex or the same sex. Then there's Jess, who identifies as genderqueer and expresses their identity through a mix of traditionally masculine and feminine clothing, rejecting the binary norms that society often imposes.

Despite the richness of these identities, numerous myths deserve to be debunked. A common one is the confusion between bisexuality and pansexuality, where bisexuality is erroneously viewed as exclusive to male and female genders. In reality, bisexuality encompasses attraction to more than one gender, not just two. Another prevalent misconception is that non-binary identities are a 'trend' or 'phase.' This not only invalidates the person's identity but also overlooks the historical presence and recognition of non-binary people in many cultures worldwide.

These clarifications are not just about semantics—they are crucial for understanding and respecting each individual's true self. This knowledge empowers us to navigate our social worlds more effectively and to advocate for ourselves and others in spaces that may not yet fully understand the spectrum of human identity. By embracing and educating about these nuances, we foster a more inclusive and empathetic community where everyone can thrive without the pressure to conform to outdated norms.

Intersectionality in Focus: Race, Disability, and Socioeconomic Status

Let's discuss a crucial concept when considering the varied experiences within our LGBTQ+ community: intersectionality.

Coined by Kimberlé Crenshaw, a leading scholar in critical race theory, intersectionality refers to the way different aspects of a person's social and political identities combine to create different modes of discrimination and privilege. Imagine an intersection of multiple roads—each road represents different identity markers like race, gender, disability, and class. Where they meet, they overlap; at this juncture, an individual can experience compounded forms of discrimination or privilege.

This framework helps us understand that their sexual orientation or gender identity does not just shape an LGBTQ+ individual's experience but is also profoundly influenced by their race, disability, and socioeconomic status. For instance, a Black transgender woman may face not only transphobia and sexism but also racism, which can affect her in unique ways that a white cisgender gay man might never encounter. These layered experiences complicate the kinds of discrimination faced and the strategies needed for advocacy.

The concept of double discrimination becomes clear when we consider LGBTQ+ individuals with disabilities. These community members often face barriers that are not just about accessibility in terms of physical spaces but also accessibility in terms of understanding and acceptance within the LGBTQ+ community itself. For example, a gay man with a physical disability might find it challenging to participate in social events at bars or clubs that are not wheelchair accessible, which are often central spaces for community gathering and support.

Socioeconomic status also plays a critical role in shaping the experiences of LGBTQ+ individuals. Those from lower socioeconomic backgrounds often have less access to healthcare, including mental health services and gender-affirming treatments, which are vital for transgender and nonbinary individuals. Furthermore, they might encounter legal systems less protective of their rights or live in areas with fewer resources and community support networks. An LGBTQ+ person's ability to navigate these challenges is significantly influenced by their economic stability, which intersects with other identity factors to either compound their vulnerability or provide avenues for resilience.

To bring these concepts to life, consider the stories shared by individuals like Maria, a Latina lesbian who navigates her identity alongside challenges related to her undocumented status and poverty. Maria's story highlights the barriers she faces in accessing health services and the strength she draws from her community. Her experience underscores the importance of looking at LGBTQ+ identities through an intersectional lens, recognizing that a complex array of social, political, and personal factors shapes each person's battle for equality and acceptance.

By embracing intersectionality, we can better advocate for policies and practices that address the specific needs of the most marginalized among us, ensuring that our efforts are inclusive and effective. It compels us to look beyond single-issue solutions and consider the full scope of an individual's life, advocating for changes that uplift our entire community's diversity. Understanding and addressing these intersectional needs challenges the structures of inequality and builds a foundation for a more just and empathetic world.

The Impact of Cultural Background on LGBTQ+ Mental Health

Our identities come from many different cultural backgrounds, which can impact how we see ourselves and how others see us. For LGBTQ+ individuals, these cultural influences can play a big role in our mental health experiences. Culturally sensitive mental health services are not just beneficial; they are vital. They acknowledge the profound impact of culture on our lives and provide care that respects and integrates our diverse backgrounds. For instance, a mental health professional working with a Muslim gay man must understand the specific cultural pressures he faces, which might include familial expectations and community stigma, to provide effective support.

Cultural stigma can often act as a barrier to seeking mental health support. In many cultures, LGBTQ+ identities may be seen as deviant or immoral, leading to significant stigma not only from society at large but also from within one's family or community. This stigma can exacerbate feelings of isolation and anxiety among LGBTQ+ individuals. Studies have shown that LGBTQ+ people from cultures with strong negative attitudes towards non-heteronormative identities are at a higher risk for mental health disorders, substance abuse, and even suicide. For example, a study published in the "Journal of LGBT Youth" found that perceived stigma and discrimination significantly contributed to higher levels of depression and anxiety among LGBTQ+ adolescents from conservative communities.

Therefore, the need for cultural competence in therapy must be addressed. Mental health professionals must be trained to recognize and address the unique challenges faced by LGBTQ+

clients from diverse cultural backgrounds. This involves more than just understanding different cultural norms and values; it requires a deep empathy and willingness to learn from clients about their specific experiences and needs. Guidelines for therapists might include training on the intersection of cultural and sexual identities, strategies for addressing family and community pressures, and ways to support clients in navigating the complexities of dual identity spaces where they may not fully belong.

Promoting cultural understanding is also crucial in broadening the perspectives of healthcare providers and the broader society. It's about shifting the narrative from one of tolerance to one of celebration of diversity. This involves highlighting the challenges and the victories of LGBTQ+ individuals across different cultures. For example, while some indigenous cultures have long recognized and respected non-binary gender identities, many modern societies are still grappling with these concepts. By sharing these global perspectives, we can foster a more nuanced understanding of how cultural contexts affect the experiences and acceptance of LGBTQ+ individuals.

Through this deeper understanding, we aim to build a more inclusive world where every LGBTQ+ individual can thrive without the burden of cultural stigma or the fear of losing their cultural identity. This is not just about improving individual lives but about enriching entire communities by embracing and celebrating the diversity within them. In this way, culturally competent mental health care supports the individual and contributes to the societal change necessary for true inclusivity and equality.

Historical Contexts of LGBTQ+ Rights and Their Influence Today

Understanding the past is crucial because it shows us where we've been, helps us understand where we are now, and guides us on where we might go. The history of LGBTQ+ rights is rich with courageous figures, pivotal movements, and profound shifts that continue to shape the lives and experiences of the community today. Let's explore some historical moments and see how they connect to our issues.

The roots of the LGBTQ+ rights movement can be traced back to at least the early 20th century, though individuals lived and struggled in silence long before then. For example, the 1969 Stonewall Riots in New York City marked a significant turning point in the United States. Triggered by a police raid at the Stonewall Inn, a bar popular among the most marginalized members of the gay community, these riots catalyzed a national and, subsequently, global push towards LGBTQ+ activism. Figures such as Marsha P. Johnson and Sylvia Rivera, prominent drag queens and trans women of color, became icons of resistance. Their bravery sparked immediate protests and inspired the first pride parades, turning a moment of defiance into a growing public movement advocating for rights and recognition.

Across the pond, the UK had its milestones. The partial decriminalization of homosexuality in 1967 was a monumental legal victory, yet it was just the beginning of a long fight against discrimination. This period also saw the rise of activism, with organizations like the Gay Liberation Front that emerged in the early 1970s advocating for societal change, not just legal reforms. These movements laid the groundwork for later achievements, such as legalizing same-sex marriage.

However, progress has not been linear. The 1980s brought about a devastating setback with the HIV/AIDS epidemic, which was met with widespread stigma and inadequate government response, particularly in the United States. The epidemic disproportionately affected gay men, but it also mobilized the community in new ways. Activist groups like ACT UP (AIDS Coalition to Unleash Power) were formed to demand better medical research and treatment, and their relentless advocacy brought significant changes in public health policy and the perception of people living with HIV/AIDS.

Today, the echoes of these past struggles are visible in ongoing challenges. Despite significant advancements in legal protections in many parts of the world, issues like workplace discrimination, hate crimes, and the rights of transgender individuals remain pressing. In more than 70 countries, homosexuality is still criminalized, underscoring the global disparity in LGBTQ+ rights. Moreover, recent years have seen a troubling rise in anti-LGBTQ+ legislation in various states across the U.S., threatening to undermine decades of progress.

This historical context is crucial for today's advocacy efforts. It reminds us that rights and acceptance can never be taken for granted; they result from decades of struggle and must be actively defended. It also shows us that the fight for equality is about changing laws and transforming societal attitudes. Each victory is a step toward a more inclusive society, but each setback is a call to action, reminding us that the journey toward equality is ongoing.

As we reflect on these historical contexts, we're reminded of the resilience of the LGBTQ+ community. The victories we now celebrate came from the bravery of those who stood up against injustice, often at great personal risk. Their legacy is not just in the rights they helped secure, but in the vibrant, diverse, and global movement they inspired. Today, as we face new challenges and opportunities, their stories and successes light our path forward and remind us that change is always possible, even in the face of seemingly insurmountable odds.

Nonbinary and Genderqueer Identities: A Deep Dive

Understanding nonbinary and genderqueer identities involves recognizing that the spectrum of gender is broader and far more colorful than the traditional binary of male and female might suggest. Nonbinary refers to gender identities that do not fit within the conventional understandings of male or female. Individuals who identify as nonbinary may experience their gender as both, neither, or a combination that might fluctuate over time. Genderqueer often used interchangeably with nonbinary, can also be an identity for those who challenge binary gender norms on a cultural level, blending, bending, and crossing gender boundaries in personal expression and identity.

These concepts are not just theoretical; they are lived every day by real people whose experiences challenge the rigid frameworks often imposed by society. For example, consider Reagan (a real person whose experiences I've been privileged to learn about), who identifies as genderqueer. They present themselves in ways that reject typical gender norms—sometimes wearing dresses, other times in a suit and tie, depending on how they feel on any given day. Reagan's story is not just about clothing choices but about the daily assertion of identity in a world that often refuses to acknowledge the legitimacy of gender expression.

People identifying as nonbinary or genderqueer face numerous challenges. Legal recognition is a significant hurdle in many parts of the world, where official documents and systems enforce a gender binary through checkboxes that do not include any other options besides male or female. This can lead to issues in every interaction with institutions that require identification —from boarding a plane to applying for a job. Healthcare presents another major challenge. Nonbinary and genderqueer individuals often encounter medical systems that are ill-equipped to address their specific health needs, particularly when it comes to mental health support and gender-affirming care. Social acceptance is yet another obstacle, with persistent stigma and misunderstanding about nonbinary identities leading to discrimination, exclusion, and sometimes, tragically, violence.

Despite these challenges, the nonbinary and genderqueer community has shown incredible resilience and creativity in coping with societal pressures. Many find support and solidarity in online communities and local support groups that affirm their identities. Advocacy groups are working tirelessly to push for legal recognition and to educate healthcare providers about the needs of nonbinary individuals. For instance, organizations like the National Center for Transgender Equality in the U.S. provide resources and advocacy for expanding legal recognition and healthcare access for nonbinary people.

Moreover, resources tailored explicitly to nonbinary and genderqueer individuals are increasingly available. These include online platforms that offer advice on navigating daily life, from choosing gender-neutral clothing to dealing with legal documentation. Workshops and seminars designed to educate employers, educators, and service providers about nonbinary identities are becoming more common, helping to broaden understanding and support at community and institutional levels.

Sharing these narratives and resources aims to illuminate the challenges and celebrate the diversity and vibrancy of nonbinary and genderqueer lives. Each story of a nonbinary or genderqueer individual is a testament to the complexity and richness of human identity and an invitation to society at large to broaden its understanding of gender beyond the binary. These stories and efforts support those within the community and challenge and expand the cultural understanding of gender for everyone.

Two-Spirit Identities: Understanding Indigenous Perspectives

In North American Indigenous cultures, Two-Spirit people have important roles beyond Western gender norms. They often take on their communities' spiritual, social, and cultural responsibilities. Historically, Two-Spirit people were revered and respected within many tribal communities. They were often seen as bridges between the material and spiritual worlds due to their unique ability to understand both male and female perspectives. This role included various responsibilities, from mediators and healers to warriors and caretakers, reflecting the dynamic and integral roles Two-Spirit individuals held.

Today, the recognition and roles of Two-Spirit people vary significantly across different Indigenous communities. Some communities have revived and embraced these traditional roles, seeing them as a crucial part of cultural heritage and a source of pride within their tribes. In these contexts, Two-Spirit individuals are often involved in cultural preservation efforts, educating others about their identities' historical and contemporary significance. For instance, at powwows and other cultural gatherings, Two-Spirit people might lead ceremonies, offer traditional teachings, or advocate for the community on land rights and cultural preservation. This visibility strengthens community bonds and empowers younger generations to explore and embrace their identities without shame.

However, despite these positive developments, many Two-Spirit individuals still face significant challenges. The imposition of Western norms and values through colonization has profoundly impacted how Indigenous communities view gender and sexuality, often leading to the stigmatization of non-binary identities. This can result in Two-Spirit people experiencing a complex form of discrimination that intersects with both indigeneity and queer identity, making it difficult to participate in either the Indigenous or mainstream LGBTQ+ communities fully. For example, some Two-Spirit individuals might find themselves at the margins in LGBTQ+ spaces that predominantly reflect white, Western perspectives and may not fully understand or respect Indigenous cultural contexts.

Moreover, the erosion of traditional Indigenous cultures—often a direct result of historical oppression, forced assimilation, and ongoing systemic inequalities—poses a significant threat to the roles and recognition of Two-Spirit people within their communities. As languages and traditions continue to face the threat of extinction, the nuanced understandings of gender and identity that include Two-Spirit roles risk being lost. It's a poignant reminder that cultural preservation is not just about maintaining historical artifacts or languages. Still, it is also about sustaining the diverse ways of being that exist within a culture.

Voices from the Two-Spirit community often highlight these issues while illuminating the pathways toward resilience and recovery. Take, for example, the story of a Two-Spirit elder from the Navajo Nation, who speaks about their role in bridging the young and the old ways. They share tales of elders who quietly passed on traditions and songs that affirmed their identity, even when it was unsafe to do so openly. These stories are not just historical records; they are lifelines that connect Two-Spirit people to their ancestors and guide them in their ongoing efforts to heal and strengthen their communities.

In their own words, "It's about weaving the old with the new. We are not relics of the past; we carry our history in our spirits and our bodies, and we move forward by sharing our truths." This perspective underscores the dynamic and evolving nature of Two-Spirit identities, reflecting the deep roots in Indigenous cultural traditions and the contemporary struggles and achievements of living Two-Spirit people. It's a powerful reminder that understanding and supporting Two-Spirit individuals is an ongoing process that requires sensitivity to both the historical and present-day contexts in which these communities live.

This dialogue between past and present, tradition and innovation, is where the strength of Two-Spirit people truly shines. It's where they reclaim the narratives that have been suppressed or forgotten and where they forge new paths for recognition and respect within and beyond their communities.

As we listen to these voices and learn from their experiences, we are reminded of the broader struggles for justice and equity facing Indigenous and LGBTQ+ communities. It's a call to action for all of us, regardless of our backgrounds, to support these efforts and to recognize the vital role that Two-Spirit people play in the cultural, social, and spiritual life of their communities. Through this understanding and support, we can contribute to a world that values and celebrates the vast diversity of human experience.

TWO

Mental Health Strategies Tailored for LGBTQ+ Needs

Navigating the complexities of mental health can often feel like trying to find your way through an intricate maze—especially for LGBTQ+ youth, where every corner and turn might present unique challenges that their heterosexual peers rarely encounter or even consider. This part of our discussion focuses on understanding and addressing the mental health needs specific to LGBTQ+ adolescents, a group that disproportionately grapples with anxiety and depression. We'll break down these challenges to understand them better and find ways to create stronger support systems and more care.

Addressing Anxiety and Depression in LGBTQ+ Youth

Understand the Prevalence

Recent studies starkly highlight that LGBTQ+ youth face significantly higher rates of anxiety and depression compared to their heterosexual counterparts. For instance, research from

The Trevor Project in 2020 indicated that 40% of LGBTQ+ respondents seriously considered attempting suicide in the past twelve months, with more than half of transgender and nonbinary youth having seriously considered it. These numbers aren't just statistics; they represent the experiences of young people struggling to find their place in a world that often seems unwelcoming or outright hostile.

Identify Contributing Factors

So, what feeds into this heightened risk? It's a tangle of various factors, each exacerbating the other. Bullying remains a prevalent issue, with LGBTQ+ students often facing targeted harassment not just from peers but, distressingly, from adults who should be in roles of trust and guidance. Family rejection is another profound source of pain—being pushed away by loved ones for one's identity can lead to profound feelings of isolation and worthlessness. Then there's the internalized stigma, where societal prejudices seep into one's self-perception, often manifesting as internal conflicts about one's worth and identity.

These elements create an environment where anxiety and depression can take root and flourish, making it crucial to address these issues with empathy, understanding, and proactive support.

Implement Targeted Interventions

How can we intervene effectively as a community of caregivers, educators, and mental health professionals? School-based programs that promote LGBTQ+ inclusivity and mental health education are vital. These programs not only support LGBTQ+ youth but also educate their peers and dismantle pervasive myths and stigmas. Family therapy that includes education about LGBTQ+ issues can also be instrumental. It can help families move from rejection to acceptance and support, creating a familial environment where LGBTQ+ youth can thrive.

For instance, implementing comprehensive school counseling programs that include training on LGBTQ+ issues can significantly mitigate feelings of isolation and distress. Educators and counselors trained in these areas become invaluable allies, capable of recognizing early signs of mental health struggles and intervening in informed and affirming ways.

Promote Support Networks

The power of community cannot be overstated. Peer support groups and online communities provide essential spaces where LGBTQ+ youth can connect with others who share similar experiences. These platforms offer more than just social connections—they are vital for reinforcing one's sense of identity and belonging. Organizations like GLSEN (the Gay, Lesbian & Straight Education Network) provide resources for starting school-based clubs, such as Genders & Sexualities Alliances (GSAs), which can serve as powerful support networks for LGBTQ+ students.

Moreover, online platforms specifically catering to LGBTQ+ youth can be a lifeline for those in geographically isolated areas or restrictive environments. Through these digital spaces, young people can find friendship, acceptance, and access to resources and information that may be unavailable in their immediate physical surroundings.

By weaving together these strategies—understanding the prevalence, addressing contributing factors, implementing targeted interventions, and promoting robust support networks —we create a multifaceted approach that not only supports LGBTQ+ youth in navigating their mental health challenges but also empowers them to thrive in all aspects of their lives. This holistic approach is not just about tackling issues as they arise but about preventing them from taking root in the first place, fostering an environment where LGBTQ+ youth feel valued, understood, and supported.

Gender Dysphoria: Clinical Insights and Personal Narratives

Understanding gender dysphoria involves delving into both the clinical landscape and the deeply personal experiences of those who live with it. Gender dysphoria is a term used by healthcare professionals to describe the psychological distress that results when a person's gender identity does not align with the sex they were assigned at birth. The Diagnostic and Statistical Manual of Mental Disorders, Fifth Edition (DSM-5), specifies certain criteria for diagnosing gender dysphoria, which include a marked incongruence between one's experienced or expressed gender and the gender others would assign them, lasting at least six months. This condition might manifest through a strong desire to be rid of one's primary and secondary sex characteristics, a strong desire for the primary and secondary sex characteristics of the other gender, and a strong desire to be of another gender or some alternative gender different from one's assigned gender.

For many, receiving this diagnosis is not just a clinical label; it is a moment of validation and an important step towards aligning their external life with their internal sense of self. Personal narratives from individuals like Robin, a trans man who first experienced gender dysphoria at a young age, illustrate the relief and validation that can come with a formal diagnosis. Robin shares, "For years, I felt like I was living inside a shell that wasn't mine. Getting diagnosed was terrifying but also incredibly freeing. It was the first step towards becoming myself on the outside and inside." Stories like Robin's underscore the complex interplay of emotions—fear, relief, validation—that accompany the journey of living with and managing gender dysphoria.

Regarding treatment, options are as diverse as the individuals seeking them. Treatment may include psychological counseling, hormone therapy, and various surgical interventions, all aimed at aligning one's physical self with one's gender identity. Psychological counseling often plays a pivotal role, providing a supportive space to explore one's gender identity, navigate the challenges associated with gender dysphoria, and plan steps toward transition, if desired. Hormone therapy can also be a transformative treatment, helping to align one's secondary sexual characteristics with one's gender identity, which, for many, is a critical aspect of alleviating dysphoria.

However, access to these treatments is not always straightforward. Many face substantial barriers, such as finding healthcare providers who are knowledgeable and affirming of transgender identities. The healthcare system, often rigid in its understanding of gender, can be a labyrinth for those seeking gender-affirming treatment. Insurance coverage is another significant hurdle; not all plans cover the costs associated with hormone therapy or gender-affirming surgeries, leaving many to face hefty out-of-pocket expenses. Moreover, societal stigma continues to cast a long shadow, with some individuals facing outright discrimination from healthcare providers or within the medical system at large.

These challenges are daunting, yet they are met with resilience and resourcefulness by the transgender and gender-nonconforming community. Online and in-person support networks are crucial in sharing information about affirming providers, navigating insurance complexities, and offering emotional support throughout seeking care. Advocacy organizations work tirelessly to push for broader insurance coverage and for the adoption of more inclusive healthcare policies that respect and accommodate the needs of transgender and nonbinary individuals. Through these collective efforts, the landscape is slowly but surely shifting towards greater understanding and acceptance, paving the way for those who come after to have a smoother path in their transitions. As we continue to listen to and elevate these personal stories, they enrich our understanding and foster a more empathetic and informed society that upholds the dignity and rights of all individuals, regardless of gender identity.

Suicide Prevention and Intervention in LGBTQ+ Populations

Let's take a moment to reflect on a sobering reality: the risk of suicide attempts and ideation among LGBTQ+ individuals is alarmingly high, particularly within the transgender and nonbinary communities. Recent data from the National Center for Transgender Equality reveals that nearly 40% of transgender adults have attempted suicide in their lifetime—nearly nine times the attempted suicide rate in the general U.S. population. These aren't just numbers; they represent countless individuals who feel so cornered by their circumstances that they see no other escape.

A myriad of factors unique to the LGBTQ+ community compounds the risks. Discrimination can erode a person's sense of worth and belonging over time, whether overt or subtle. Non-acceptance from families, peers, and broader social networks forces many to hide their true selves, amplifying feelings of isolation and loneliness. Then there's minority stress —the chronic social stress experienced by members of stigmatized minority groups—which can be particularly insidious. It's not just about facing bigoted remarks or unfair treatment; it's about the constant vigilance and emotional labor involved in navigating a world that often doesn't understand or accept LGBTQ+ identities.

Addressing these challenges requires a multifaceted approach. Effective suicide prevention strategies must go beyond general mental health support to address the specific needs of the LGBTQ+ community. This includes crisis intervention services that are not only accessible but are also affirmatively knowledgeable about LGBTQ+ issues. For instance, The Trevor Project operates a 24/7 suicide prevention hotline specifically for LGBTQ+ youth, offering a lifeline to those feeling lost or hopeless.

Community-based programs play a crucial role as well. These initiatives provide safe spaces where LGBTQ+ individuals can find support and connection. These programs help mitigate many's isolation by fostering a sense of community. Moreover, they can offer tailored workshops and support groups that address the unique challenges faced by LGBTQ+ individuals, helping them develop coping strategies and resilience in the face of adversity.

Advocacy for better mental health resources is also crucial. This means pushing for more research into LGBTQ+ mental health issues, advocating for policies that protect against discrimination, and ensuring that mental health professionals are trained to address the specific challenges faced by LGBTQ+ clients. It's about creating a healthcare system that serves and understands the needs of the LGBTQ+ community.

Resource Guide

To support you or someone you know in times of crisis, here's a list of resources that can offer help and hope:

- **The Trevor Project**: Offers crisis intervention and suicide prevention services to LGBTQ+ youth. Available 24/7 at 1-866-488-7386 or via chat and text.
- **Trans Lifeline**: A grassroots hotline and microgrants organization offering direct emotional and financial support to trans people in crisis. For the hotline, call 877-565-8860.
- **LGBT National Help Center**: This center provides confidential peer support and information on local resources for all ages. The hotline is 1-888-843-4564.
- **Crisis Text Line**: Text "LGBTQ" to 741741 to connect with a trained crisis counselor who can provide immediate support and information about further resources.

These hotlines and programs provide immediate crisis support and connect individuals to ongoing support and communities. They are vital components in the broader effort to prevent suicide among LGBTQ+ populations, offering hope and a reminder that no one has to face their darkest moments alone. Through these resources and the continued efforts of advocates and communities, there is a path forward—a chance for renewal and resilience even in the face of profound challenges.

Coping with Minority Stress: Tools and Techniques

When we talk about the stress that comes uniquely with being part of a marginalized group, we're diving into what's known as the minority stress model. This model helps us understand how societal stigma, prejudice, and discrimination don't just float around in the ether; they have real, palpable effects on individuals. For LGBTQ+ people, this means navigating a world that often doesn't see them, doesn't understand them, or worse, openly rejects them. This persistent and pervasive stress doesn't just go away after a difficult interaction or a bad day. It's the kind of stress that follows you.

Managing this stress requires more than the usual stress relief techniques because the source of the stress is continuous and deeply rooted in societal structures. Mindfulness practices, for instance, can be a powerful tool here. Mindfulness isn't just about calming the mind; it's about becoming aware of your thoughts and feelings without judgment. For someone facing minority stress, mindfulness can help unpack feelings of internalized stigma or anticipate stressors in a controlled, safe environment. Techniques could include guided meditations, mindfulness exercises tailored explicitly to recognizing and managing feelings of rejection or alienation, and even simple breathing exercises designed to ground and center oneself in acute stress.

Cognitive-behavioral strategies are another cornerstone in managing minority stress. These strategies involve identifying negative, often automatic thought patterns that can spiral out of control and lead to anxiety or depression. For LGBTQ+ individuals, these might be thoughts like "I will never be accepted" or "I am wrong for being who I am." Cognitive-behavioral therapy helps reframe these thoughts into something more positive and realistic, providing a mental toolkit for handling situations where stigma and discrimination arise. It's about changing the narrative in your head so that it doesn't amplify the stress the world throws at you.

Self-care routines also play a critical role. But here, self-care isn't just bubble baths and scented candles—it's about creating routines that affirm one's identity and provide respite from societal pressures. This could look like setting boundaries around consuming media that might trigger negative feelings, engaging in physical activities that help connect body and mind positively, or dedicating time to hobbies and interests that reinforce a sense of self-worth and joy. It's about carving out spaces and activities that remind you that you are more than the discrimination you face.

Community involvement is both a buffer against and an antidote to minority stress. Being part of an LGBTQ+ community or network provides critical social support, which research shows can mitigate the effects of minority stress. These communities provide a sense of belonging, reduce feelings of isolation, and offer practical support and understanding that might be lacking elsewhere. They can be spaces of joy and celebration where individuals can express their true selves freely and fully. Moreover, community involvement often includes advocacy work, which not only works to change the societal conditions that create minority stress but also gives individuals a sense of agency and purpose.

This advocacy work is crucial because it aims at the root of minority stress: societal stigma and systemic discrimination. Advocating for policy changes that protect LGBTQ+ rights, increase awareness and understanding of LGBTQ+ issues, and promote inclusion can eventually reduce the stressors that LGBTQ+ people face daily. This means supporting efforts to pass non-discrimination protections, promoting positive representations of LGBTQ+ individuals in the media, and supporting educational programs that tackle homophobia and transphobia from an early age.

The fight against minority stress is both deeply personal and unavoidably political. By engaging in these practices and pushing for broader societal change, you are not only looking after your mental health but also contributing to a future where such intense levels of minority stress are no longer a common part of the LGBTQ+ experience. Through individual resilience and collective action, the weight of this stress can be lifted, piece by piece, until the burden is no longer yours, or anyone's, to bear alone.

Building Resilience in Transgender and Nonbinary Individuals

Resilience might often be pictured as the ability to bounce back from challenges, but for transgender and nonbinary individuals, it's deeply woven into the very fabric of everyday existence. It's about more than recovery; it's about thriving in an environment that frequently questions your identity and rights. Resilience for someone who is transgender or nonbinary involves cultivating a profound sense of self-worth and empowerment amid societal challenges. It's a dynamic mix of self-acceptance, community support, and the strength to advocate for one's rights and well-being.

The cornerstone of building resilience is fostering strong community ties. The value of finding a community that resonates with your experiences cannot be overstated. Such communities provide social support and a platform for sharing experiences and strategies for navigating the complexities of life as a transgender or nonbinary person. For instance, local LGBTQ+ centers often host groups where individuals can meet others with similar experiences. These settings provide a space to feel understood without explanation, help normalize experiences, and reduce feelings of isolation. Furthermore, online forums and social media platforms have emerged as vital spaces for those who may not have physical access to supportive communities, offering connections and resources that can be pivotal in building resilience.

Engagement in advocacy is another powerful resilience-building strategy. Advocacy might involve activities ranging from participating in local LGBTQ+ rights campaigns to larger-scale efforts like lobbying for policy changes that protect and recognize transgender and nonbinary rights. Such engagement contributes to societal change and reinforces an individual's sense of agency and self-worth. It turns personal challenges into a narrative of empowerment and action, helping individuals to see themselves as active architects of their lives and communities. Moreover, being part of advocacy efforts often provides a sense of purpose and connection, further reinforcing community ties and personal resilience.

Accessing affirming mental health care is crucial. Mental health professionals who are not only supportive but also educated in the unique experiences of transgender and nonbinary individuals can make a significant difference. Such professionals can provide guidance tailored to navigating gender dysphoria, societal rejection, or family issues, which are common among transgender and nonbinary populations. Therapy can be a safe space to explore one's identity, cope with discrimination, and develop strategies for building and maintaining resilience. It's important that mental health providers not only affirm their clients' gender identity but also understand the complex ways in which societal pressures affect mental health.

Role Models and Mentors

The importance of role models and mentors in fostering resilience cannot be understated. Seeing someone who shares aspects of your identity thrive can be incredibly affirming. Role models in the transgender and nonbinary community often provide living proof that despite the challenges, one can lead a fulfilling and successful life. They also offer practical insights and wisdom gained from navigating similar paths. Mentors, formally through programs or informally within community settings, can offer guidance, support, and understanding invaluable for personal growth and resilience.

Consider the story of Paul, a nonbinary professional who mentors young transgender individuals. Paul shares both career advice and their experiences navigating personal and professional challenges. Their mentorship helps mentees understand that they are not alone in their struggles and that it is possible to overcome them. This kind of relationship can be transformative, offering hope and practical strategies to those just beginning to find their way in their identity and society.

Navigational Tools

Practical navigational tools are essential for dealing with societal challenges. Coping with misgendering, for example, requires both internal resilience and external strategies. It might involve setting clear boundaries with peers and colleagues or preparing responses for possible scenarios. Handling discriminatory practices might involve knowing one's rights in the workplace or healthcare settings and being prepared to advocate for oneself or seek legal assistance if necessary.

Maintaining mental and emotional health amidst these challenges involves regular self-care practices tailored to individual needs. These might include routines that affirm one's gender identity, such as engaging with supportive communities online or in person, or activities that promote mental and emotional well-being, such as mindfulness exercises, arts, or physical activities that help express oneself and relieve stress.

By weaving together these strategies—fostering community ties, engaging in advocacy, accessing affirming care, finding role models, and utilizing practical tools—transgender and nonbinary individuals can build resilience as a shield against adversity and as a foundation for a vibrant and fulfilling life. This resilience is dynamic and continuously developed through experiences and interactions within supportive and challenging environments. It offers a way to navigate the world with confidence and pride in one's identity, transforming personal journeys into stories of empowerment and advocacy.

Addressing Substance Use in LGBTQ+ Communities

Substance use often casts a long shadow over many communities. Still, for those in the LGBTQ+ community, the interplay of unique social stressors and personal experiences can significantly elevate the risk and impact. Diving into the prevalence, reports suggest that LGBTQ+ individuals are more likely to use alcohol, tobacco, and other substances than their heterosexual counterparts. This elevated use isn't just a statistic; it reflects the complex interplay between societal pressures and personal coping mechanisms that many in the community navigate daily.

Assess the Scope

To understand the scope, let's look at the numbers. Studies have consistently shown that gay, lesbian, bisexual, and transgender individuals engage in substance use at higher rates than the general population. For example, according to data from the National Survey on Drug Use and Health, adults defined as "sexual minority" (i.e., those who identify as lesbian, gay, or bisexual) were more than twice as likely to have used illicit drugs in the past year compared to their heterosexual peers. This data doesn't just highlight a disparity; it underscores the need for targeted responses that address why these rates are higher.

Understand Underlying Causes

The root causes of increased substance use among LGBTQ+ individuals often stem from trying to cope with the stressors imposed by living in a less-than-accepting society. Discrimination, stigma, and the daily battles with acceptance can lead many to seek escape from substances. Past traumas, which are unfortunately common in the LGBTQ+ community due to higher rates of violence and emotional abuse, also play a critical role. These traumatic experiences can leave lasting scars, and without proper support and coping mechanisms, turning to substance use can seem like a viable short-term solution.

Treatment Programs

Recognizing the specific needs of LGBTQ+ individuals, several treatment programs have been designed to provide not just recovery assistance but also a space that affirms their identity and addresses the root causes of substance use. These programs often incorporate elements of trauma-informed care, recognizing the high prevalence of past trauma in the community. They also emphasize the importance of creating a supportive environment that respects and celebrates sexual orientation and gender identity, which can significantly affect recovery outcomes.

One such program, the Pride Institute, is dedicated to providing a healing space that addresses the specific psychological and social needs of LGBTQ+ individuals. Their approach is not just about treating substance use but also about fostering an environment where individuals can explore aspects of their identity that may have contributed to their substance use. This holistic approach recognizes the intertwined nature of identity, trauma, and recovery, offering a more comprehensive and effective treatment model.

Prevention and Education

Prevention and education are crucial in addressing substance use within the LGBTQ+ community. These efforts need to go beyond general drug education to tackle the specific issues that may lead LGBTQ+ individuals to substance use. This means creating safe spaces where young people can discuss their pressures and challenges. These education programs specifically address coping mechanisms and resilience and public health campaigns that destigmatize both substance use disorders and LGBTQ+ identities.

Schools, community centers, and online platforms are pivotal in these preventative efforts. They can offer programs and workshops that not only educate about the dangers of substance use but also provide real tools for dealing with discrimination, building healthy relationships, and fostering self-esteem. For example, a workshop might focus on building skills for resilience and emotional regulation, helping LGBTQ+ youth develop healthier ways to cope with stress and discrimination.

By addressing substance use from these multiple angles—understanding its prevalence, tackling the underlying causes, offering affirming treatment programs, and emphasizing targeted prevention and education—we can better support LGBTQ+ individuals in not just surviving but thriving, free from the burdens of substance misuse. This multifaceted approach helps individuals and strengthens the community, building a foundation where future generations can find better support and fewer reasons to turn to substances in the first place.

Moving forward, the lessons learned here about the complexity of substance use within LGBTQ+ communities can inform broader discussions and actions in the subsequent chapters. As we continue to explore mental health interventions and community support mechanisms, we carry with us a deeper understanding of the challenges and the best strategies to address them, ensuring that every member of the LGBTQ+ community has the opportunity to lead a healthy, fulfilling life. This foundation sets the stage for continued exploration of mental health challenges and the robust community responses that can transform lives.

THREE

Navigating Family and Societal Interactions

Navigating the complex layers of family and societal interactions can often feel like trying to speak a language you've never been taught — especially when it involves coming out as LGBTQ+. This chapter peels back those layers, offering heartfelt guidance and practical strategies to navigate these potentially turbulent waters gracefully and authentically. Coming out is a profound act of self-disclosure that can reshape your relationships and significantly impact your mental and emotional health. Here, you'll find strategies and a compass to guide you through this personal evolution, acknowledging the diverse dynamics you might face within your family and broader social circles.

Coming Out: Strategies for Diverse Family Dynamics

Understand the Spectrum of Reactions

Coming out can stir a spectrum of reactions, from heartfelt acceptance to painful rejection and everything in between. Each family's dynamics are unique and influenced by cultural, religious, and personal values that shape their view of the world and, consequently, their reaction to your coming out. It's crucial to prepare for a range of responses. Some family members might embrace you with open arms, seeing your truth as a testament to your trust in them. Others might respond with confusion or distress, influenced by misconceptions or deeply ingrained prejudices. And in some cases, you might encounter outright rejection, a response that can be devastating.

Preparing for these outcomes involves bracing yourself emotionally and understanding that their reactions do not reflect your worth but rather their beliefs and experiences. It can be helpful to strategize each possible reaction, discussing your plan with a therapist or a trusted friend who can offer perspective and support. This preparation doesn't just equip you to handle difficult reactions; it also helps reinforce your emotional resilience, ensuring that you're grounded in your truth no matter the response.

Tailored Coming Out Strategies

The approach to coming out can significantly affect the outcome, and tailoring your strategy to your family's dynamics can make the process smoother. Consider the general atmosphere of your home: Is it open and communicative, or more reserved and private? For liberal or open-minded families, a direct conversation might be the best approach. In contrast, with conservative or religious families, you might choose a more gradual disclosure, providing them with resources and time to understand.

Timing and setting are also crucial. Choosing a moment of calm, perhaps during a quiet evening at home, can foster a more reflective and intimate discussion than in a public setting or during a family crisis. If safety is a concern, consider having these conversations in a neutral place where you feel secure or having a support person present. Remember, your safety and well-being should always come first.

Psychological Preparation

Mental and emotional preparation before coming out is essential. Building resilience and preparing psychologically can help you navigate this challenging process. Consider engaging in reflective practices like journaling about your fears and hopes regarding coming out or practicing conversations with a counselor or in a support group. This preparation helps solidify your resolve and clarifies your reasons for coming out, equipping you with the emotional strength to handle a range of reactions.

Visualizing positive outcomes can also be a powerful tool. Imagine scenarios where your family responds with love and acceptance. Such visualizations can ease anxiety and create a psychological blueprint for success, helping you approach the conversation with optimism and confidence.

Support Systems

Having a robust support system is invaluable when you decide to come out. This network can include close friends, supportive family members, counselors, or members of an LGBTQ+ support group. These individuals can offer emotional support, practical advice, and a safe space to express feelings. They can also serve as your sounding board, helping you refine your approach to coming out and being there to debrief after you've taken this significant step.

Online communities can also be a significant source of support, especially if you feel isolated in your immediate environment. Platforms like Reddit, Tumblr, or specialized forums provide access to a global community of individuals who have gone through similar experiences. They can offer encouragement, share their stories, and provide insights relevant to your situation.

Building and maintaining these support systems helps you through the process of coming out and enriches your journey. They provide a network of relationships built on understanding, respect, and mutual support. These connections remind you that while the path of authenticity can be challenging, you do not have to walk it alone. With the right strategies and support, you can navigate your coming out process to honor your truth while considering the dynamics of your relationships, turning a potentially daunting endeavor into a journey of self-affirmation and growth.

Dealing with Rejection: Emotional Support and Practical Advice

Facing rejection from family, friends, or society is a harsh reality that many in the LGBTQ+ community confront. It's painful, often leaving deep emotional scars, yet it's a hurdle you may navigate with a blend of resilience and resourcefulness. Here, we explore tangible coping mechanisms and strategies for maintaining your emotional health and relationships, even in the face of stark rejection.

Coping with rejection starts with recognizing its impact on your mental health and seeking appropriate support. Engaging in therapy can be a transformative step. A therapist who specializes in LGBTQ+ issues can offer a safe space to process feelings of rejection and develop strategies to cope with them effectively. Therapy can help you understand and frame your experiences in a way that fosters healing rather than resentment. Additionally, leaning into supportive communities plays a crucial role. Whether these are local LGBTQ+ groups, online forums, or close friends who affirm your identity, these networks can offer comfort and understanding that mitigate rejection. The shared experiences can remind you that you're not alone, providing solace and practical advice on navigating similar challenges.

Self-care is another cornerstone of coping with rejection. This practice goes beyond the occasional indulgences and encompasses everyday actions that nurture mental, emotional, and physical health. Setting aside time each day to engage in activities you love, ensuring you eat well, get enough sleep, and stay active. It's about making deliberate choices to take care of your well-being, reinforcing the idea that you are worthy of care and love, especially when others suggest otherwise.

Building emotional resilience is crucial in surviving and thriving despite rejection. This involves developing a deep, enduring sense of self-worth that isn't reliant on the acceptance of others. Practices like mindfulness can be incredibly helpful here. Mindfulness encourages a state of active, open attention to the present. When you're mindful, you observe your thoughts and feelings from a distance without judging them as good or bad. This practice can help you detach from harmful self-criticism and catastrophic thinking, which are often exacerbated by experiences of rejection. Similarly, affirmations can reinforce your sense of self-worth. Regularly affirming your values and rights to love and acceptance can fortify your psyche against negative messages from those who reject your identity.

Navigating complex relationships with family members who are initially unsupportive requires a delicate balance of empathy and self-preservation. Setting boundaries is essential; it involves communicating your needs and limits. These boundaries include topics of conversation that you find disrespectful or harmful or how frequently you engage with someone who struggles to accept your identity. Gradual engagement can be effective, too, allowing space and time for your family members to process their feelings and come to a place of understanding, guided by gentle but firm conversations. It's important to gauge progress and adjust your strategies to protect your emotional well-being.

Knowing your legal rights and the resources available is crucial for those facing severe rejection or discrimination. Many countries and local jurisdictions offer legal protections against discrimination based on sexual orientation and gender identity. Familiarizing yourself with these laws can empower you to advocate for yourself when discrimination arises. Legal advocacy groups and LGBTQ+ organizations often provide resources and guidance for navigating these legal landscapes. They can offer support in workplace discrimination, housing discrimination, and other legal challenges you might face.

Numerous social and legal resources are available to those experiencing rejection. Hotlines, counseling services, and crisis centers can provide immediate support. Organizations like the Human Rights Campaign and Lambda Legal offer tools and information on rights and protections in various scenarios, including dealing with family law issues, discrimination, and civil rights abuses in both personal and professional settings.

Navigating rejection is undeniably challenging, but you can emerge resilient and empowered with the right tools and support. By embracing self-care, seeking supportive communities, and utilizing available resources, you can protect your well-being and maintain meaningful connections, even in adversity. Remember, the path to self-acceptance and acceptance by others—is often a journey of many steps, some forward and some back, but always toward a future where you can live authentically and freely.

Creating Chosen Families and Supportive Networks

The concept of chosen families holds a special place in the heart of the LGBTQ+ community. For many, especially those estranged from their biological families due to misunderstanding or outright rejection, chosen families represent a sanctuary of acceptance and understanding. A chosen family is not defined by blood or traditional societal structures but by bonds of unconditional support and affection. These relationships are often forged between friends, mentors, and peers who understand the journey of an LGBTQ+ individual intimately. The value of these families lies not just in the comfort they offer but in their capacity to empower and affirm one's identity, which can be particularly vital in a world that often questions or negates LGBTQ+ experiences.

Building such a network, however, involves more than finding people; cultivating deep, meaningful connections that stand the test of time and challenge. The first step is contacting your local or online LGBTQ+ community and engaging in community events, whether social gatherings, support group meetings, or volunteer opportunities. This can open doors to meeting others sailing in the same boat. Online platforms offer many resources, from forums and social media groups to dating apps that facilitate friendship and support networks. These spaces can be particularly helpful in areas where the LGBTQ+ community isn't visible or accessible.

Once you start forming connections, fostering these relationships requires effort and empathy. It's about more than just spending time together; it involves actively listening to each other's experiences, providing emotional support, and celebrating each other's victories, no matter how small. For example, attending a friend's art show or offering a comforting ear during tough times can strengthen your bond, creating a mutual sense of loyalty and support.

Encouraging active participation in these relationships is crucial. Creating a chosen family sometimes means initiating gatherings or check-ins, especially when your group members feel isolated or overlooked. Organizing regular meet-ups, whether virtual or in-person, can help maintain the sense of community and connectedness that defines a chosen family. These gatherings don't always need to be large or elaborate; even small, intimate meetups can provide a sense of belonging and safety.

Maintaining these relationships over time requires good communication skills, mutual respect, and understanding of each other's boundaries. Open and honest communication helps prevent misunderstandings and builds trust, making it easier to support each other during difficult times. It's also important to recognize and celebrate the diversity within your chosen family, understanding that each member may have different needs and ways of expressing themselves. This can involve learning about and respecting various cultural backgrounds, personal histories, and individual identities, which enriches the relationship and deepens the connection.

Conflicts are inevitably part of any relationship, and chosen families are no exception. Handling conflicts with care and consideration can strengthen these bonds rather than weaken them. This might involve developing conflict resolution skills like active listening, empathy, and non-confrontational communication. It's about finding common ground and resolving disagreements, affirming each person's feelings and perspectives.

Cultivating a chosen family is a dynamic process that evolves as you and your family members grow and change. These networks not only provide a buffer against the challenges faced by LGBTQ+ individuals but also enrich your life, offering joy, companionship, and a shared understanding. They remind you that family isn't always defined by who you're born to but rather by who you choose to love and support. As you build and nurture these relationships, you create connections that support you and help form a stronger community and sense of belonging.

Navigating LGBTQ+ Identity in Conservative Regions

Living as an LGBTQ+ individual in a conservative region can sometimes feel like walking a tightrope, balancing the need for authenticity with the need for safety. In such areas, prevailing attitudes and cultural norms might not only be unsupportive but actively hostile towards LGBTQ+ identities. These environments often harbor a strong adherence to traditional values where anything that deviates from the norm is either invisibilized or met with resistance. Understanding this landscape is crucial for navigating it effectively and, more importantly, safely.

The first step is to gauge the general sentiment of your local community toward LGBTQ+ issues. This can involve observing local laws, media portrayals of LGBTQ+ topics, public events, and people's general behavior toward diversity and inclusion. In conservative regions, LGBTQ+ identities might be met with negative stereotypes or religious condemnation, which can permeate everyday interactions and influence everything from family dynamics to workplace culture. Awareness of these attitudes allows you to anticipate potential challenges and plan your actions accordingly, including how openly you express your identity.

Strategies for maintaining personal safety and mental well-being are vital in these settings. Discretion can sometimes be a necessary tool. For instance, you may be more selective about whom you come out to or opt to express your identity in more subtle ways that feel safer. Online platforms can provide a discreet yet powerful means of connecting with supportive communities. These digital spaces often offer anonymity and a broader network of support than might be available locally. They allow you to explore your identity, share experiences, and receive advice without the immediate risks of doing so in public or semi-public physical spaces.

Finding or creating safe spaces is another critical strategy. This might involve identifying LGBTQ+ friendly businesses, organizations, or events known for their inclusivity. Consider starting a secret or private support group where such resources are scarce. This could be as simple as a monthly meet-up at a trusted person's home or a private online group where members can share and connect securely. These spaces can serve as vital sanctuaries where you can be yourself without fear, fostering a sense of community and belonging that bolsters your mental health and emotional resilience.

Advocacy and rights awareness are essential in conservative regions. Educating yourself about your legal rights is crucial in protecting yourself from discrimination and harm. Many countries and regions have laws that protect against discrimination based on sexual orientation and gender identity, even if the local cultural climate is unsupportive. Knowing these rights can empower you to advocate for yourself in situations where you might face discrimination, such as in housing, employment, or healthcare.

Moreover, becoming an advocate can also mean joining or forming alliances to achieve greater acceptance and legal protections for LGBTQ+ individuals in your area. This could involve organizing awareness campaigns, participating in local government meetings, or collaborating with national LGBTQ+ organizations to bring attention to the issues faced by the community in conservative regions. While advocacy can be challenging, it can also lead to significant changes that improve the lives of LGBTQ+ individuals locally and beyond.

Navigating life as an LGBTQ+ individual in a conservative region requires a blend of caution, courage, and creativity.

Understanding the local cultural landscape, strategically seeking safety, forming supportive connections, and advocating for your rights can create a pathway that honors your identity and well-being. These strategies not only serve to protect you but also pave the way for greater acceptance and change, contributing to a future where being yourself no longer requires a tightrope walk.

Interfaith Dialogue: LGBTQ+ Perspectives and Religious Communities

Navigating the delicate intersection of LGBTQ+ identity and religious beliefs can feel like walking a tightrope, especially in traditions where doctrine seems at odds with the reality of LGBTQ+ lives. However, fostering dialogue between LGBTQ+ individuals and their religious communities can not only bridge gaps but can also illuminate common grounds of understanding and compassion. Initiating these conversations requires tact, respect, and a genuine willingness to understand differing viewpoints. It's about creating a safe space where faith and identity are respected, allowing for an exchange that can enrich both sides of the conversation.

When engaging in these dialogues, one effective strategy is to find allies within the religious community who may already be supportive or open to LGBTQ+ issues. These allies can act as bridges, helping to facilitate discussions and lend legitimacy to the perspectives and experiences of LGBTQ+ members. It's also beneficial to approach the dialogue focusing on shared values such as love, compassion, and justice—principles often central to religious teachings. By framing LGBTQ+ rights within the context of these shared values, you can appeal to the moral teachings that resonate deeply within the religious community, potentially fostering greater empathy and openness to understanding.

Moreover, educational sessions that involve sharing personal stories from LGBTQ+ individuals can be profoundly impactful. These narratives can humanize issues that might otherwise be abstract or misunderstood, providing concrete examples of how certain doctrines or attitudes affect the lives of real people. These stories not only spark empathy but also provide a starting point for deeper discussions about how religious communities can support their LGBTQ+ members. For instance, inviting LGBTQ+ speakers to religious gatherings or events can provide a platform for these important stories to be shared and heard.

Navigating religious doctrine is another significant aspect of these interfaith dialogues. Many LGBTQ+ individuals struggle with the perceived conflict between their spiritual beliefs and their identity. Guiding reconciling these can be a crucial aspect of support. This often involves looking at religious texts through different interpretative lenses. Many religious texts have been interpreted in various ways over the centuries, and highlighting interpretations that advocate for inclusion and acceptance can offer comfort and validation to LGBTQ+ individuals who wish to remain part of their religious communities.

Engaging with open-minded religious leaders can also be instrumental in this process. Leaders willing to engage in dialogue and reconsider traditional interpretations can be powerful allies. These leaders can influence their congregations and foster an environment of greater acceptance and understanding within the religious community. Workshops or seminars that educate religious leaders about LGBTQ+ issues, conducted by theologians specializing in progressive interpretations of religious texts, can effectively broaden understanding and promote inclusivity.

Supportive religious networks and groups that embrace LGBTQ+ members are vital, as they provide spaces where individuals can explore their religious beliefs and identities without compromise. Highlighting these networks can not only offer direct support to LGBTQ+ individuals but also serve as models for other religious groups striving to become more inclusive. For example, many Christian denominations have supportive groups like Affirming Ministries or Integrity USA, which advocate for including LGBTQ+ people within the church. Similarly, in the Jewish community, organizations like Keshet promote LGBTQ+ inclusion in all facets of Jewish life. Showcasing these examples can inspire other religious groups to take similar steps toward inclusion.

Lastly, educational outreach within religious communities is crucial for fostering a deeper understanding and acceptance of LGBTQ+ individuals. This can involve developing educational materials that address common questions and misconceptions about LGBTQ+ issues from a faith-based perspective. Workshops, discussion groups, and even sermons that explore the intersection of faith and LGBTQ+ identity can help dispel myths and build bridges of understanding. These efforts can fundamentally alter the narrative within religious communities, shifting from exclusion to embrace.

By engaging in these multifaceted strategies, the dialogue between LGBTQ+ individuals and religious communities can move from mere coexistence to meaningful collaboration and support. This dialogue is about changing perspectives and enriching the spiritual lives of all community members, creating an inclusive environment where faith and identity are celebrated in their beautiful diversity. Through respectful conversation, open-minded interpretation, and supportive community-building, we can forge a path where religion and LGBTQ+ identities are not just compatible but harmoniously interwoven.

Aging and LGBTQ+: Challenges in Elder Communities

As we consider the full spectrum of the LGBTQ+ experience, we must focus on an often-overlooked segment of our community: our elders. Aging as an LGBTQ+ individual comes with a unique set of challenges. Many of our elders face isolation not just from the general community but sometimes from younger members of the LGBTQ+ community as well. Discrimination in elder care facilities remains a significant concern, as these environments can often be less progressive than society. Additionally, many LGBTQ+ elders do not have children and may be estranged from family members, which can lead to a lack of familial support as they age.

Isolation can be particularly pronounced for LGBTQ+ elders who may not have the same support networks available as their heterosexual counterparts. This isolation can be exacerbated by the loss of partners and peers, leading to significant emotional distress. Elder care facilities, which should be safe havens, can sometimes be places where LGBTQ+ elders face discrimination or must hide their identities to avoid conflict. This is not just about hurt feelings; it affects the quality of care received and can lead to depression, anxiety, and a decreased will to engage in daily activities.

Advocating for inclusive policies in elder care is crucial to combat these challenges. This advocacy can take many forms, from training staff on LGBTQ+ issues to implementing non-discrimination policies that explicitly include sexual orientation and gender identity. Creating inclusive policies helps ensure LGBTQ+ elders receive the respect and care they deserve. It's also about setting a standard that care should be compassionate and inclusive across the board—not just in specialized facilities.

Building and maintaining support networks for LGBTQ+ elders is equally important. These networks can include peer support groups, both in-person and online, that connect LGBTQ+ elders. These groups provide social interaction and mutual support and can significantly reduce feelings of isolation. They can also be a source of practical support, offering information and resources on navigating the challenges of aging as an LGBTQ+ person.

Legal and healthcare planning is another area where LGBTQ+ elders face unique challenges. Many are concerned about who will make medical decisions for them if they become incapacitated and whether their wishes will be respected. Legal tools such as wills, powers of attorney, and advanced healthcare directives protect their rights. Furthermore, healthcare planning must also consider the specific needs of LGBTQ+ elders, which may include finding LGBTQ+ friendly providers who understand and respect their identities.

Supporting our LGBTQ+ elders involves recognizing their unique challenges and taking active steps to address them. It's about ensuring they are safe, cared for, valued, and respected within our community. By advocating for inclusive care, building robust support networks, and ensuring proper legal and healthcare planning, we can significantly improve the quality of life for LGBTQ+ elders.

As we close this chapter on navigating family and societal interactions, we've explored the diverse challenges and enriching solutions within the LGBTQ+ community's complex fabric. From coming out to dealing with rejection, creating chosen families, and ensuring the well-being of our elders, each section has woven together the threads of experience, strategy, and hope. As we move forward, let's carry these insights into our continued exploration of LGBTQ+ experiences, fostering a deeper understanding and stronger advocacy across all aspects of life.

FOUR

Advocacy and Legal Rights

Imagine stepping into a room where the rules are unclear, the language is unfamiliar, and yet every decision made in this room significantly affects your life. This is often what navigating the legal landscape feels like for many in the LGBTQ+ community. Understanding your rights, the shifts in legal protections, and learning to stand up for yourself in legal situations can transform this confusing landscape into a map you can confidently navigate. This chapter is about arming you with that knowledge and the tools to advocate effectively for yourself and others.

Understanding Your Legal Rights as an LGBTQ+ Individual

Identify Key Rights

Your journey through the maze of legalities begins with knowing your fundamental rights. Every LGBTQ+ individual has the right to privacy, freedom from discrimination, and access to healthcare—rights that are enshrined in various international human rights treaties and national laws. In the United States, for example, the Civil Rights Act and various state laws protect against discrimination based on sexual orientation and gender identity in employment, housing, and public accommodations. Similarly, in healthcare, the Affordable Care Act prohibits discrimination based on gender identity and sexual orientation. Knowing these rights is the first step to ensuring you are treated fairly and can lead a life without discrimination.

Changes in the Legal Landscape

The legal landscape regarding LGBTQ+ rights is constantly evolving, marked by significant victories and, at times, frustrating setbacks. For instance, the landmark U.S. Supreme Supreme Court ruling in 2015 that legalized same-sex marriage nationwide was a monumental victory for LGBTQ+ rights. However, the journey continued. More recent challenges include issues surrounding transgender rights, such as the right to use public facilities that match one's gender identity or the ongoing battles against so-called "bathroom bills." These legal battles highlight the ongoing struggle for equality and underscore the importance of staying informed about the latest developments in legal protections for the LGBTQ+ community. A timeline of such landmark cases and legislation can help us appreciate the hard-won progress and understand the contours of the battles ahead.

Resource Guide

Navigating the legal system can be daunting, but you don't have to do it alone. There are numerous resources available to help.

Organizations like the ACLU (American Civil Liberties Union), Lambda Legal, and the Transgender Law Center offer legal assistance and can guide you through the complexities of the legal system. These organizations provide direct legal support and champion policy changes that advance LGBTQ+ rights nationally. Additionally, many local LGBTQ+ advocacy groups offer resources and support for dealing with legal issues. Keeping a list of these resources handy can provide you with quick access to expert advice and support when you need it most.

Self-Advocacy Tips

Self-advocacy is a powerful tool. It begins with understanding how to document instances of discrimination or rights violations. Keeping detailed records of such incidents, including dates, times, and descriptions of what occurred, can be crucial if you decide to pursue legal action. Knowing where to seek legal counsel is also key. Many legal organizations provide directories of LGBTQ+ friendly lawyers who are well-versed in LGBTQ+ legal issues. Moreover, educating yourself about your rights and the legal obligations of employers, healthcare providers, and public institutions can empower you to speak up confidently and effectively when facing discrimination.

Navigating the legal landscape as an LGBTQ+ individual involves a blend of knowledge, resources, and proactive advocacy. By understanding your rights, staying informed about legal changes, utilizing available resources, and embracing self-advocacy, you can protect yourself and contribute to the broader fight for equality and justice within the LGBTQ+ community. This empowerment through legal knowledge is not just about navigating the system; it's about changing it, one informed, confident step at a time.

Strategies for Grassroots Advocacy and Community Organizing

Grassroots advocacy represents the heartbeats of local communities channeling their collective energies into voices that demand change. At its core, grassroots advocacy in the LGBTQ+ community amplifies those voices that might otherwise be overshadowed or ignored. It thrives on the local level, where activists understand the nuances of their communities and can tailor their strategies to meet specific needs and challenges. This approach brings about change and fosters a sense of empowerment among community members, as they see tangible results from their direct actions.

Organizing effective community events, demonstrations, or campaigns starts with clearly understanding your goals. Are you raising awareness, influencing policy, or providing support? Once the goals are set, the next steps involve meticulous planning and broad community engagement. Start by gathering a small, committed team to help coordinate efforts. Diverse teams with individuals from various community sectors can offer multiple perspectives and strengthen your planning process. Utilize local community centers, social media platforms, and community bulletin boards to spread the word and gather support. When planning events or demonstrations, consider the logistics like location, timing, necessary permits, and safety measures to ensure everything runs smoothly.

Engagement continues beyond event planning. Effective advocacy requires reaching out to participants and keeping them involved. Provide clear, actionable steps that individuals can take beyond attending an event, such as signing petitions, contacting local representatives, or volunteering for related causes. Follow-up is crucial, so keep the community informed about the event's outcomes and the next steps. This not only maintains momentum but also helps build a sustained advocacy movement.

Building coalitions with other marginalized communities can significantly amplify your advocacy efforts. These alliances can draw on shared experiences of discrimination and a mutual interest in achieving equality and justice. Start by identifying potential community partners who share similar goals or have supported LGBTQ+ rights in the past. Reach out to these groups and propose collaborative projects or events that address common issues. When building these coalitions, it's essential to approach them with respect and openness, acknowledging each group's unique experiences and perspectives. Regular meetings and open communication channels can help align goals and strategies, ensuring that all voices are heard and valued. Practical tips for effective collaboration include joint fundraising events, co-authored public statements, and shared resources for campaign materials.

One inspiring example of successful grassroots advocacy is the campaign led by transgender activists to gain legal recognition for non-binary genders. In Oregon, this campaign involved years of lobbying, community engagement, and legal challenges, culminating in the state legally recognizing non-binary as a gender option on driver's licenses and state IDs in 2017. This victory not only marked a significant legal advancement for transgender rights in the U.S. but also provided a powerful model for similar advocacy efforts nationwide. The success of this campaign was largely due to the persistent efforts of grassroots activists who organized community support and worked in coalition with legal organizations to challenge discriminatory policies.

The power of grassroots advocacy lies in its ability to mobilize local communities and create change from the ground up. By understanding the principles of grassroots activism, organizing impactful events, building strong coalitions, and learning from successful case examples, you can significantly advance LGBTQ+ rights in your community and beyond. Remember, every big change starts with small, local actions. Your efforts can spark a movement that leads to lasting change, reinforcing that when communities unite for a cause, their collective voice can achieve incredible milestones.

Navigating Legal Systems: Resources and Advice

Navigating the legal system can sometimes feel like trying to understand a complex new language, especially when it comes to LGBTQ+ issues that span various layers of legislation—from local ordinances to federal statutes. Let's break it down: at the local level, you might encounter city or county laws that address specific issues like anti-discrimination policies in housing or employment. Moving up a notch, state laws can widely vary, with some states offering broad protections for LGBTQ+ individuals, while others may unfortunately have few or no such protections. At the highest level, federal laws provide overarching guidelines and protections, although these too can change depending on the political climate and judicial interpretations.

Understanding this tiered system is crucial because it helps you identify which laws apply to your situation and where you can seek recourse if your rights are challenged. For instance, state laws offer more immediate and relevant protections if you face workplace discrimination than waiting for a federal ruling. However, if you're dealing with issues like marriage or immigration, which are governed by federal law, understanding these statutes becomes essential.

Finding an LGBTQ+ friendly lawyer or legal advocate can significantly ease the process when facing challenges within the legal system. Not all lawyers are familiar with or sensitive to LGBTQ+ issues, so it's important to seek out professionals who specialize in this area or are known community allies. Organizations like the National LGBT Bar Association offer directories of legal professionals who advocate for LGBTQ+ rights and have expertise in relevant areas of the law. Engaging a lawyer who understands the nuances of LGBTQ+ legal issues provides you with better representation and ensures your lawyer is fully invested in your fight for justice and equality.

Protective legislation plays a pivotal role in safeguarding the rights of LGBTQ+ individuals. Laws such as the Equality Act, which seeks to provide comprehensive protections for LGBTQ+ people across key areas of life, including employment, housing, credit, education, public spaces and services, federally funded programs, and jury service, are essential. Understanding these laws allows you to navigate better situations where you might face discrimination. For example, knowing that the Equality Act prohibits discrimination based on sexual orientation and gender identity in employment can empower you to challenge unfair practices in your workplace.

Engaging effectively with legal professionals is more than just hiring a lawyer; it's about building a partnership that empowers you to advocate for your rights. When meeting with a lawyer, come prepared with all relevant documents and a clear outline of your issues. Being honest and detailed about your situation lets your lawyer provide the best advice and representation. It's also important to communicate your expectations and to understand the legal process you are embarking on. Ask questions about anything you're unsure of, from legal terms to procedural steps, and ensure you're kept in the loop about the progress of your case. Remember, a good legal professional understands the law and how to communicate it in a way that makes you feel informed and supported.

Navigating the legal system as an LGBTQ+ individual involves understanding the multi-layered structure of laws that affect you, seeking specialized legal assistance, knowing your protective rights, and engaging proactively with legal professionals. By arming yourself with this knowledge and these strategies, you transform from being a passive participant in the legal system to an informed advocate for your rights and well-being. This empowerment through legal understanding is about tackling immediate legal challenges and shaping a more just and equitable system that upholds the dignity and rights of all LGBTQ+ individuals.

Case Studies of Successful LGBTQ+ Advocacy

Inspirational Stories

The landscape of LGBTQ+ advocacy is dotted with remarkable stories of resilience and triumph, each illuminating the pathways through which dedicated individuals and groups have catalyzed significant change. One compelling example is the transformation achieved by the advocacy group *Equality Now*, which played a pivotal role in overturning anti-LGBTQ+ legislation in a small, conservative town. The group, led by a charismatic trans woman named Elisa, began by organizing town hall meetings to discuss the impacts of discriminatory laws on the LGBTQ+ community. These meetings were initially met with resistance, but persistence led to a breakthrough when local business leaders, moved by personal stories shared at the meetings, became vocal supporters of the cause.

Elisa and her team employed various advocacy techniques, from peaceful protests and partnerships with legal advocates to media campaigns highlighting inclusive policies' economic and social benefits. The turning point came when they facilitated workshops with local legislators, helping them understand the legal and ethical implications of anti-LGBTQ+ laws. The campaign culminated in the repeal of the town's discriminatory statutes, a victory that not only improved the lives of local LGBTQ+ individuals but also served as a blueprint for similar efforts in other regions. This case study highlights the power of local engagement and the importance of building alliances across diverse community segments, turning potential adversaries into allies.

Diverse Tactics

Effective advocacy often requires a multifaceted approach, adapting strategies to fit each situation's unique contexts and challenges. In the case of *Trans Rights Now*, a group dedicated to advancing healthcare rights for transgender individuals, the tactics ranged from legal challenges to public awareness campaigns. The group's initial focus was on challenging a healthcare policy that denied necessary medical treatments for trans people through strategic litigation. At the same time, they launched an educational campaign aimed at healthcare providers, illustrating the medical necessity and human rights dimensions of transgender healthcare.

Parallel to these efforts, the group engaged in a storytelling project, sharing video testimonials of transgender individuals detailing their healthcare challenges and triumphs. These stories were shared on social media platforms, gaining widespread attention and fostering greater public empathy and support for trans healthcare rights. The combination of legal action, educational outreach, and personal storytelling created a comprehensive advocacy approach that addressed the issue from multiple angles, ultimately leading to policy changes that enhanced healthcare access for transgender individuals across the state.

Lessons Learned

Each advocacy campaign offers valuable lessons that can guide future efforts. One key takeaway from the story of Equality Now is the importance of localizing advocacy efforts to fit each area's specific cultural and social context. Understanding the unique dynamics of the community you are engaging with can inform more effective strategies and messaging. Additionally, the success of *Trans Rights Now* underscores the effectiveness of combining legal strategies with grassroots storytelling. This approach amplifies the message and humanizes the issues, making the abstract legal and policy discussions more relatable and urgent to the broader public.

Another critical lesson is the importance of resilience and adaptability in advocacy work. Change often comes slowly, and setbacks are inevitable. The ability to adapt your strategies in response to new challenges and to persist despite obstacles is crucial. This resilience, coupled with a strategic understanding of when and how to push for change, can determine the success of advocacy efforts.

Impact Assessment

Evaluating the impact of advocacy efforts is essential for measuring success and understanding how to improve future campaigns. The repeal of anti-LGBTQ+ legislation in the town where *Equality Now* was active led to measurable improvements in the mental health and well-being of LGBTQ+ residents, as evidenced by local health surveys. Additionally, the increased visibility of LGBTQ+ issues fostered a more inclusive community atmosphere, which attracted diverse residents and businesses, boosting the local economy.

In the case of *Trans Rights Now*, the impact extended beyond the immediate policy changes. The campaign brought significant attention to transgender healthcare issues, encouraging medical institutions across the nation to reevaluate their policies and practices regarding transgender patients. This broader cultural shift towards more inclusive healthcare practices highlights the far-reaching effects that focused, well-executed advocacy can have, extending well beyond the campaign's immediate goals.

These case studies celebrate past successes and serve as a blueprint for ongoing and future advocacy efforts. They remind us that in the fight for LGBTQ+ rights, every action counts, and even small wins contribute to the larger goal of equality and justice for all. As we continue to advocate for change, these stories of past victories provide both inspiration and instruction, guiding us through the complexities of advocacy with lessons forged in the fires of earlier battles.

Advocating for Inclusive Policies in Educational Institutions

When you walk through the halls of a school or university, the policies that govern these spaces might not be immediately visible, but their impact is deeply felt, especially by LGBTQ+ students and staff. Currently, the landscape of educational policies varies widely. Some institutions have robust anti-discrimination policies and inclusive curriculums that acknowledge and support LGBTQ+ identities. In contrast, others lag, lacking basic protections that can make educational environments feel unsafe or unwelcoming for LGBTQ+ individuals. These policies, or the lack thereof, can significantly affect students' and staff's mental health, academic performance, and overall well-being.

Effective advocacy strategies are essential to shift this landscape towards greater inclusivity. One powerful approach is advocating for the inclusion of non-discrimination clauses in school policies. These clauses should explicitly prohibit discrimination based on sexual orientation and gender identity in all areas of the educational experience, from admissions and hiring practices to student services and extracurricular activities. Additionally, advocating for inclusive curricula is crucial. This means pushing for integrating LGBTQ+ histories, cultures, and contemporary issues into the curriculum across disciplines, not as optional content but as integral parts of the educational framework. This inclusion benefits LGBTQ+ students by reflecting on their experiences, validating their identities, educating the broader student body, and fostering a more accepting and knowledgeable community.

Engaging effectively with decision-makers is key to driving these changes. This engagement can take many forms, from formal meetings with school boards or university administrations to participating in public forums or serving on educational committees. When preparing for these interactions, it's important to come equipped with not just passion but also data and concrete examples that illustrate the benefits of inclusive policies—not only for LGBTQ+ individuals but for the entire educational community. Presenting evidence from research that links inclusive environments to better overall student outcomes can be particularly persuasive. Additionally, sharing personal stories or testimonials from those affected by current policies can provide powerful illustrations of the need for change.

Support networks within educational settings, such as Gender and Sexuality Alliances (GSAs), are pivotal in advocating policy changes. GSAs, or similar groups, provide safe spaces for LGBTQ+ students and allies to unite, support one another, and organize around issues affecting their community. These groups can be instrumental in raising awareness about the importance of inclusive policies and generating student-led advocacy efforts. By organizing events, speaking at school meetings, and collaborating with other student organizations, GSAs can mobilize a broad support base and pressure educational leaders to implement necessary changes.

Advocating for more inclusive educational policies is not just about changing specific rules or guidelines but about transforming the educational culture so that all members of the LGBTQ+ community can thrive. Through strategic advocacy, engaging decision-makers, and fostering strong support networks, we can create educational environments that accept and celebrate all identities. This transformative effort not only enhances the lives of LGBTQ+ students and staff but enriches the entire educational community by fostering an atmosphere of diversity, equity, and inclusion.

Workplace Rights and How to Advocate for Them

Navigating the workplace as an LGBTQ+ individual often involves more than just managing job responsibilities. Understanding your rights under national and state labor laws is crucial, as these laws are designed to protect you from discrimination based on your sexual orientation or gender identity. For instance, the U.S. Equal Employment Opportunity Commission (EEOC) enforces federal laws that make it illegal to discriminate against a job applicant or an employee because of the person's race, color, religion, sex (including pregnancy, transgender status, and sexual orientation), national origin, age (40 or older), disability or genetic information. Many states and localities have enacted similar protections, and some have provisions specifically protecting LGBTQ+ people.

However, knowing your rights is just the first step. Creating an inclusive workplace goes beyond legal compliance; it fosters an environment where all employees, regardless of their sexual orientation or gender identity, can feel safe and valued. Advocating for inclusive policies, such as gender-neutral bathrooms and inclusive health benefits, can significantly impact the daily experiences of LGBTQ+ employees. To initiate these changes, consider forming or joining a diversity and inclusion committee at your workplace. These groups can work directly with human resources to implement policies that reflect the needs and rights of LGBTQ+ employees. Additionally, organizing training sessions on LGBTQ+ inclusivity can educate your coworkers and management about these policies' importance, helping shift workplace culture towards greater acceptance and understanding.

Discrimination, unfortunately, still occurs, and knowing how to handle it is imperative. If you face discrimination at your workplace, document every incident with as much detail as possible, noting dates, times, and witnesses. Reporting these incidents to your human resources department is a critical next step. If your workplace needs an HR department, or if the response from HR needs to be improved, consider seeking legal recourse. Contacting organizations such as Lambda Legal or the ACLU can guide you on proceeding, ensuring your rights are fully protected and advocated for.

Allies play an indispensable role in advocating for LGBTQ+ rights in the workplace. If you are an ally, educate yourself about the challenges LGBTQ+ colleagues may face and take active steps to support them. This can include everything from speaking out against discriminatory remarks to supporting or leading inclusivity initiatives in your workplace. Allies can also help amplify LGBTQ+ voices in meetings or discussions where those voices might be marginalized or overlooked, ensuring that LGBTQ+ employees have equal opportunities to contribute and advance.

Creating an inclusive workplace where everyone can thrive involves a collaborative effort. By understanding your rights, advocating for inclusive policies, handling discrimination appropriately, and fostering strong alliances, you can help transform your workplace into a supportive environment for all employees. This not only benefits LGBTQ+ individuals but also enhances the overall productivity, creativity, and morale of the entire workforce, proving that inclusivity is not just a legal requirement or a moral obligation but a profound opportunity to enrich every aspect of our professional lives.

In wrapping up this chapter on workplace rights and advocacy, we've explored the multifaceted approach needed to ensure that LGBTQ+ individuals can navigate their professional environments safely and successfully. From understanding legal rights to fostering inclusive workplace policies and handling discrimination, each aspect plays a crucial role in shaping a work environment where everyone's dignity and rights are respected. As we move forward, let these insights inspire you to advocate for change for yourself and the broader LGBTQ+ community, ensuring that every workplace can become a diversity, equity, and inclusion model.

FIVE

Healthcare and Wellness

I magine navigating a city without a map, where every turn feels uncertain and every path uncharted. This metaphor often mirrors the experience many transgender and nonbinary folks face when seeking to affirm healthcare—a journey fraught with obstacles but also one of profound importance and potential transformation. In this chapter, we'll guide you through finding gender-affirming care, preparing for your appointments, understanding your treatment options, and advocating for your health needs confidently and clearly.

Finding Gender-Affirming Care: A Step-by-Step Guide

Identify Affirming Providers

Finding healthcare providers who are not only knowledgeable but also genuinely supportive of transgender and nonbinary health needs can feel like a daunting task. Yet, it's a critical first step in your healthcare journey. Start by tapping into online directories that list LGBTQ+ friendly healthcare providers. Organizations such as GLMA (Health Professionals Advancing LGBTQ Equality) and the World Professional Association for Transgender Health (WPATH) provide searchable databases of providers trained in and sensitive to the specific needs of the LGBTQ+ community.

Another invaluable resource is your local LGBTQ+ community. You can contact community centers, support groups, and even online forums, where members often share their experiences with specific providers. These personal recommendations can be incredibly helpful as they offer insights and nuances you might not find in a professional listing.

First Appointment Preparation

Preparing for your first appointment is crucial once you've identified a potential provider. Create a checklist of essential things to bring, such as medical records and a list of medications you take. Preparing questions to assess the provider's experience and sensitivity to gender-affirming care is also helpful. These questions could include inquiries about their familiarity with hormone therapies, their approach to trans health, and examples of how they've supported other trans and nonbinary patients. Remember, this appointment is as much about them meeting your standards as it is about assessing your health.

Understanding Treatment Options

Understanding the range of medical interventions available is essential in making informed decisions about your health care. Gender-affirming treatments can include hormone replacement therapies (HRT), surgeries such as top surgery or gender confirmation surgery, and non-surgical options like voice therapy. Each treatment option has its considerations, potential risks, and benefits. Providers should clearly explain these details, allowing you to weigh each option based on your health goals and medical history. They should also discuss the expected timelines for these treatments, as understanding the duration and stages of therapy can help you manage expectations and plan your life accordingly.

Advocating for Yourself

Advocating for yourself in a healthcare setting is a powerful affirmation of your right to respectful and appropriate care. It involves clear communication of your health concerns and needs. If you ever feel dismissed or misunderstood, it's important to assert your concerns or seek a second opinion. Additionally, familiarize yourself with your legal rights as a patient. In many places, laws protect you from discrimination based on gender identity or expression. Knowing these rights can empower you to advocate for yourself effectively, especially when you might need to challenge discriminatory practices or policies.

Navigating the healthcare system as a transgender or nonbinary person involves several layers of complexity, from finding the right provider to understanding and choosing between different treatment options. However, by utilizing resources wisely, preparing thoroughly for healthcare visits, and learning to advocate effectively for your needs, you can transform this process into a more navigable and empowering experience. As you continue to engage with healthcare providers, remember that your journey is yours alone—unique in its challenges and opportunities for growth and self-affirmation.

Mental Health Care: Ensuring Competence in LGBTQ+ Issues

When we talk about competence in mental health care for LGBTQ+ individuals, we're addressing more than just a basic understanding of general psychological principles. It requires a nuanced grasp of the unique challenges that you, as a member or ally of the LGBTQ+ community, may face. This includes understanding the impacts of minority stress, the complexities of gender identity, and the effects of societal discrimination, which are often intertwined with mental health issues. A competent therapist recognizes these layers and is equipped not only with the knowledge but also with the empathy to address them effectively.

Finding a therapist who embodies this competence might seem daunting, but there are steps you can take to ensure you find the right match. Start by seeking therapists who clearly state their experience with or specialize in LGBTQ+ issues on their profiles. Many therapists include their qualifications and areas of expertise in psychology-related directories like Psychology Today. During your initial consultation, consider asking them about their training and experience working with LGBTQ+ clients. Questions might include, "Can you share how you've supported transgender clients in the past?" or "What is your approach to dealing with issues related to sexual orientation and gender identity?" Their answers can give you insight into their level of understanding and their ability to empathize with and effectively treat LGBTQ+ individuals.

In terms of therapeutic models, several have been found particularly effective in addressing the mental health needs of LGBTQ+ individuals. Affirmative therapy, for instance, is a model that not only recognizes but also addresses the negative influences of societal prejudice on an individual's mental health and well-being. This type of therapy validates and supports LGBTQ+ identities and relationships in a positive and affirming manner, actively working against existing biases and discrimination that LGBTQ+ individuals can internalize. Cognitive-behavioral therapy (CBT) has also been adapted for LGBTQ+ clients to help address issues like anxiety and depression, helping to reframe negative patterns of thought and behavior that may be rooted in experiences of stigma and discrimination. Furthermore, group therapy can be a powerful tool, providing a space where individuals can share experiences and strategies for coping with challenges in a supportive environment, reinforcing that they are not alone in their struggles.

Building a therapeutic relationship based on trust and mutual respect is key to effective therapy. It's important for you to feel understood and validated in your identity and experiences. A strong therapeutic relationship involves open communication, where you feel comfortable sharing your thoughts and feelings without fear of judgment. It also requires transparency from your therapist about the therapeutic process and mutual agreement on goals and expectations. Remember, therapy is collaborative; you actively participate in your healing journey. If at any point you feel that your therapist is not providing the support you need, it's okay to seek out someone else who might be a better fit. Therapy is very personal; the right match is crucial to your mental health and well-being.

Navigating mental health care as an LGBTQ+ individual involves understanding what comprises competent care, knowing how to find the right therapist, being aware of effective therapeutic models, and building a relationship with your therapist that is based on trust and mutual understanding. By taking these steps, you can empower yourself with the support you need to face life's challenges, knowing that your mental health is handled with the care and respect it deserves.

Sexual Health Education Tailored for LGBTQ+ Needs

When you think about sex education, you might recall sitting in a classroom, uncomfortably shifting in your seat as a teacher outlined the mechanics of reproduction. For many, especially within the LGBTQ+ community, traditional sex education often feels disconnected from the realities of your experiences and needs. It's like having a map showing only a fraction of the terrain. Comprehensive sex education aims to address this gap by inclusively covering a range of topics relevant to all sexual orientations and gender identities, not just the heterosexual and cisgender perspectives typically highlighted.

The necessity for comprehensive sex education in schools and communities cannot be overstated. It goes beyond the basics of how bodies work; it's about equipping you with knowledge about your body, rights, and emotional health. It covers consent, respect, relationships, and the specific health considerations of LGBTQ+ individuals, which are often sorely lacking in traditional curricula. For instance, navigating relationships and intimacy can significantly impact your mental and emotional well-being. Furthermore, this type of education helps dismantle stigmas and myths surrounding LGBTQ+ sexualities and identities, fostering a more inclusive and understanding society.

Now, let's talk about safe sex practices, which are crucial for protecting your health but are often not discussed in the context of LGBTQ+ experiences. Knowing about and having access to appropriate protection methods like condoms, dental dams, and PrEP (pre-exposure prophylaxis for HIV) is essential. Regular health screenings are also a key part of sexual health, yet many LGBTQ+ individuals face barriers in accessing healthcare that respects and understands their needs. Being informed about what tests are important and how often to get screened (for example, HIV testing, STI screenings, and cervical screenings for individuals with a cervix who are sexually active) can empower you to take control of your health.

Addressing common concerns specifically related to the LGBTQ+ community involves discussing topics like hormone therapy and its impact on sexual health, which is a significant concern for many transgender and nonbinary individuals. Hormone replacement therapy can affect your sexual function, fertility, and even your sexual preferences and experiences. It's important that these changes are anticipated and discussed openly with healthcare providers who are knowledgeable and sensitive to the nuances of transgender health. Another common concern is the risk of STIs and how to engage in safer sex practices that respect your body and identity.

To support your journey in understanding and navigating sexual health, numerous resources and networks are available. Organizations like Planned Parenthood offer not only reproductive health care but also resources specifically tailored to LGBTQ+ individuals, including hormone therapy and tailored sexual health education. Websites like Scarleteen provide inclusive and comprehensive sex education resources online. Additionally, many LGBTQ+ community centers offer workshops and support groups that focus on sexual health topics, providing a space to learn and discuss these issues in a safe and supportive environment.

Empowering yourself with knowledge and resources on sexual health can transform the way you navigate your health and wellness. It's about having the right information at the right time, enabling you to make informed decisions that respect your body and identity. As you continue to explore and understand more about your sexual health, remember that you are entitled to care, respect, and support that acknowledges and celebrates who you are.

Navigating Health Insurance and LGBTQ+ Care

Understanding the intricacies of health insurance is crucial, especially when it concerns the LGBTQ+ community, where healthcare needs can be unique and sometimes complex. When you're looking at health insurance options, it's important to know exactly what kind of coverage is offered, particularly regarding transgender and nonbinary health services, which are often overlooked or inadequately covered. Start by carefully reviewing the policy details, including the fine print that lists exclusions and limitations. Some insurance policies may have specific stipulations or require pre-authorizations for gender-affirming procedures. Look for policies that explicitly cover gender-affirming surgeries, hormone therapies, and other related medical needs without extensive exclusions. Additionally, it's beneficial to choose providers with a track record of handling claims for LGBTQ+ individuals respectfully and efficiently, ensuring that your interactions are free from discrimination.

One of the recurrent challenges you face is the denial of coverage for gender-affirming treatments. Insurance companies sometimes categorize these necessary medical procedures as cosmetic or elective, which can lead to claims being unjustly denied. Knowing the legal avenues to challenge such decisions is vital in these situations. Many regions have legal protections in place that require insurance companies to cover medically necessary treatments for transgender individuals, including hormone therapy and surgical procedures. If you encounter a denial, the first step is to file an appeal directly with your insurance provider. Document all interactions meticulously and be prepared to provide medical evidence that underscores the necessity of the treatment. If the appeal is denied, you can escalate your case to the state insurance commissioner's office, which can offer further recourse depending on your location.

Advocating for more inclusive and comprehensive insurance policies is another critical step. This can involve everything from participating in community advocacy efforts to change public policies to directly negotiating with your employer or insurance providers to expand coverage options. When discussing policy improvements with insurers or employers, arm yourself with data and personal testimonies highlighting the need for comprehensive transgender-inclusive health policies. Showing how inclusive policies benefit individuals and can lead to better overall health outcomes and reduced long-term healthcare costs can be persuasive.

Alternative funding sources can be a lifeline for those without comprehensive insurance or who find that necessary treatments are not covered. Many community organizations and advocacy groups offer grants specifically designed to help cover the costs of hormone therapy and surgeries for transgender and nonbinary individuals. Additionally, some healthcare providers offer sliding-scale payment options based on income, which can make treatments more affordable. Crowdfunding has also become a popular method to cover medical expenses, with platforms like GoFundMe used to raise funds for gender-affirming surgeries. While these options should not have to be a substitute for comprehensive insurance coverage, they can provide necessary support in the interim.

Navigating health insurance effectively requires a thorough understanding of your policy's specifics, being prepared to challenge unjust denials, and knowing how to advocate for more inclusive coverage. It also means exploring all available options to ensure you receive the necessary care. As you manage these challenges, remember that you are not alone; many community resources and networks support you through this process, offering guidance and assistance to make your healthcare journey as smooth as possible.

Holistic Approaches to LGBTQ+ Wellness

When discussing holistic health, we look beyond immediate treatments for specific ailments. Instead, we focus on the complete picture of your well-being—encompassing physical, mental, and emotional health. This approach is particularly crucial for the LGBTQ+ community, which often navigates complex health disparities due to systemic barriers and social stigma. Holistic health aims to heal the whole person, not just to treat symptoms but to foster an overall wellness that supports a fulfilling and healthy life.

Integrative health practices are central to this holistic approach, blending traditional medical treatments with complementary therapies to achieve optimal health. For many in the LGBTQ+ community, integrating practices like yoga and meditation into their healthcare routine can significantly enhance well-being. Yoga, for example, offers both physical and mental health benefits, including reduced anxiety, improved strength and flexibility, and greater body awareness, which can be incredibly empowering for those undergoing gender-affirming transitions. Meditation, too, provides a mental space for calm and reflection, which can be a sanctuary from the stresses and anxieties that often accompany the navigation of LGBTQ+ identities.

Nutritional counseling is another integrative practice that can have profound health benefits. A balanced diet supports physical health, which is foundational, but the benefits extend beyond the physical. Nutritional wellness also plays a significant role in mental health. Foods can affect mood and energy levels, impacting everything from daily functioning to psychological resilience. A nutritionist familiar with LGBTQ+ health can tailor dietary recommendations that support hormone treatments or help manage the side effects of medications, providing a personalized approach that respects and enhances your medical care.

The effectiveness of these holistic practices hinges significantly on the cultural competency of the providers. Culturally competent healthcare providers understand the unique challenges faced by the LGBTQ+ community and are sensitive to the nuances of diverse identities and experiences. They create a welcoming environment where you can feel safe and supported in discussing all aspects of your health. When healthcare providers acknowledge and respect your identity, it fosters a therapeutic relationship that can significantly enhance the efficacy of holistic health practices. This respect and understanding are crucial in encouraging individuals to engage fully and honestly in their health care, ensuring they receive the most appropriate and effective treatments.

Creating a personal wellness plan is a proactive way to incorporate these holistic health strategies into your everyday life. Start by assessing your current health needs and goals. Are you looking to reduce stress? Improve your physical fitness? Manage a health condition more effectively? Once you've defined your goals, consider how different holistic practices might help you achieve them. A combination of meditation for stress relief, yoga for physical health, and nutritional counseling to optimize your diet. The key is to create a manageable and enjoyable plan to help you stick with it over the long term.

Incorporating holistic health practices into your life isn't about adhering to a strict regimen but finding balance and wellness that works for you. It's a dynamic process that can adapt to your changing health needs and goals, providing a supportive foundation as you navigate life's challenges and joys. As you explore these integrative practices, remember that each step you take moves toward better health and a deeper harmony between your body, mind, and spirit.

Support Systems and Therapeutic Alliances

Navigating healthcare, particularly as an LGBTQ+ individual, often requires more than just knowing where the nearest clinic is or who the best doctors are. It involves building a network of support that understands and respects your unique needs. This isn't just about having people to turn to when things get tough; it's about creating a community that actively contributes to your ongoing health and well-being. The importance of these support systems cannot be overstated—they are often the backbone of successful and sustained healthcare management, especially for those who might face barriers due to their LGBTQ+ identity.

To build this vital support network, look at the resources available within your local community. Many cities have LGBTQ+ community centers that offer support groups and connections to healthcare providers who are allies of the LGBTQ+ community. These centers can be invaluable in helping you navigate the often complex healthcare system. Additionally, consider online communities, which can be a great resource for support and advice at any time of the day. Platforms like Reddit and specialized LGBTQ+ forums provide anonymity and diverse perspectives and experiences that can help guide your healthcare journey.

Healthcare advocacy groups are another crucial element of your support system. These organizations work at the grassroots and national levels to advocate for policies that improve healthcare access and quality for LGBTQ+ individuals. By getting involved with or utilizing the resources of these groups, you can stay informed about your rights and the latest developments in LGBTQ+ healthcare. Furthermore, these groups often provide educational resources to help you better understand your healthcare needs and how to advocate for them.

Therapeutic alliances complement support systems and offer a more personalized approach to managing health. They are partnerships between you and your healthcare providers built on mutual respect and understanding. To form effective therapeutic alliances, it's important to communicate openly with your healthcare providers about your needs and concerns. Be clear about your health goals and ask about different treatment options. A provider willing to listen and respond thoughtfully to your concerns is likely a good partner in your healthcare journey.

Creating these alliances can also mean educating your providers about the specific health issues faced by the LGBTQ+ community and your personal health history. This mutual education process can help build a stronger, more effective partnership that supports your overall health and well-being.

To illustrate the positive impact of strong support systems and therapeutic alliances, consider the case of Jackson, a nonbinary individual who struggled with severe anxiety and depression. Jackson felt misunderstood and marginalized by their initial healthcare providers, which only exacerbated their mental health issues. However, after connecting with a local LGBTQ+ advocacy group, Jackson was able to find a therapist who specialized in LGBTQ+ mental health. Together, they developed a comprehensive treatment plan that addressed not only Jackson's anxiety and depression but also the stressors related to their LGBTQ+ identity. This therapeutic alliance became a cornerstone of Jackson's mental health management, providing them with the understanding and support needed to improve their mental health significantly.

The journey toward effective healthcare management is deeply personal and can vary widely from one individual to another. However, the foundational elements of building strong support systems and forming therapeutic alliances are universally beneficial. These relationships enhance one's ability to navigate the healthcare system and enrich one's overall well-being, providing a network of care that supports both physical and mental health.

In wrapping up this chapter on Healthcare and Wellness, we've explored the multifaceted approach necessary to ensure that LGBTQ+ individuals can navigate their health effectively and with dignity. From understanding the complexities of gender-affirming care to the critical role of comprehensive sexual health education and the importance of supportive networks and therapeutic alliances—each aspect plays a crucial role in shaping a healthcare experience that is respectful, informed, and empowering. As we turn the page to the next chapter, let's carry these insights forward, continuing to advocate for a healthcare system that meets the needs of all, regardless of gender identity or sexual orientation.

SIX

Educational and Workplace Inclusion

Imagine stepping into a classroom where every lesson, story, and discussion reflects a part of you, where your identity and experiences are acknowledged and valued not just in special seminars but integrated into the everyday curriculum. This vision is a dream and a goal we can achieve by developing LGBTQ+ inclusive curricula. Beyond merely adding a chapter or a sidebar about LGBTQ+ rights, this involves fundamentally rethinking how educational content can embrace a full spectrum of experiences, ensuring that every student sees themselves in the lessons they learn.

Developing LGBTQ+ Inclusive Curricula

Integrating LGBTQ+ Topics Across the Board

Integrating LGBTQ+ topics into educational curricula should not be confined to social studies or literature but woven throughout various subjects to provide a holistic representation. For instance, when teaching about civil rights in a history class, the struggles and triumphs of LGBTQ+ individuals and groups should be as prominent as those of other marginalized communities. In science classes, educators can discuss the contributions of LGBTQ+ scientists whose innovations and discoveries have been historically overlooked or minimized due to their identity.

Moreover, in health and wellness classes, it's crucial to discuss topics relevant to LGBTQ+ health openly and accurately, providing all students with a clear understanding of diverse experiences and fostering an environment of inclusivity and respect. By integrating these topics across different subjects, schools not only provide a well-rounded education but also normalize LGBTQ+ identities, counteract stereotypes, and promote a school culture of inclusiveness and acceptance.

Engaging Educators in LGBTQ+ Inclusivity Training

For curricula changes to be effective, educators must be equipped with the knowledge and sensitivity to handle LGBTQ+ topics competently. Professional development programs should include comprehensive training on LGBTQ+ issues, focusing on terminology, the historical context of the LGBTQ+ rights movement, and current issues facing the community. This training should empower educators to handle classroom discussions sensitively, promptly, and effectively manage discriminatory behavior.

It's also beneficial to involve educators in the curriculum development process. Their firsthand experience with student interactions and classroom dynamics can provide valuable insights into how best to introduce and discuss LGBTQ+ topics. This collaborative approach improves the curriculum and ensures that educators feel more confident and supported in their teaching, which can significantly enhance the classroom experience for all students.

Resource Recommendations for Inclusive Education

To support educators and enrich the curriculum, it's essential to provide a range of resources that accurately and respectfully represent LGBTQ+ perspectives. Recommended resources might include books like "Queer: A Graphic History" by Meg-John Barker and Julia Scheele, which explores queer thought and theory in an accessible format. Documentaries such as *The Death and Life of Marsha P. Johnson* offer engaging insights into significant figures in LGBTQ+ history. Multimedia tools like these can help bring lessons to life and provide varied perspectives that enrich students' understanding.

Educational tools specifically designed for younger audiences, like the picture book *And Tango Makes Three*, about a same-sex penguin couple, can be particularly effective in teaching inclusivity from an early age. Providing a curated list of such resources ensures educators can access quality materials to help them integrate LGBTQ+ content effectively and sensitively.

Feedback and Adaptation: Ensuring the Curriculum Meets Student Needs

To ensure that the curriculum genuinely serves the needs of LGBTQ+ students and fosters an inclusive environment, it's vital to establish mechanisms for ongoing feedback from both students and staff. Schools should regularly solicit this feedback through surveys, focus groups, and open forums, encouraging honest communication about how effectively the curriculum addresses LGBTQ+ topics and where improvements are needed.

This feedback loop should not be a mere formality but a critical component of the curriculum development process. By actively seeking and responding to input from LGBTQ+ students and allies, schools can continuously adapt their educational approaches to meet the evolving needs of their student populations. This adaptive approach enhances the learning experience and demonstrates a genuine commitment to inclusivity and respect for all students' identities.

Creating an LGBTQ+ inclusive curriculum is about more than adding content; it's about transforming educational environments into spaces where all students, regardless of their identity, can learn and grow with dignity. This commitment to inclusivity in education not only benefits LGBTQ+ students but enriches the entire school community, fostering a culture of understanding, respect, and celebration of diversity. As we continue to push for these changes, let's envision and work towards a day when every student can see themselves reflected in their education, feeling valued and supported in their learning journey.

Safe Spaces in Education: Best Practices

Creating safe spaces in educational settings is not just about carving out a small corner where LGBTQ+ students can feel secure. It's about cultivating an environment where every student knows they are seen, understood, and valued. A safe space is a place of refuge and respect that actively counters the isolation and discrimination that LGBTQ+ students might face. It's where students can express themselves freely, explore their identities, and receive support without judgment or fear. This nurturing environment is crucial for student's well-being and academic success and fosters a broader culture of inclusiveness and respect within the school community.

Implementing Effective Safe Space Strategies

When discussing implementing safe spaces, we're looking at a proactive approach that involves several layers, starting with the physical environment. Designating specific classrooms or areas within the school as safe spaces is a significant first step. These areas should be visible to all students as places where they can find support and safety. Inside. The space can be equipped with resources like books and materials that reflect and celebrate LGBTQ+ identities, along with contact information for external support services like hotlines or counseling centers.

However, creating a safe space goes beyond the physical setup; it requires cultivating an environment where students feel genuinely protected and supported. This involves establishing and enforcing robust anti-bullying policies that explicitly include protections for LGBTQ+ students. Schools need to make it clear that harassment and discrimination are not tolerated and that there are strict consequences for such behaviors. Training for students and staff on recognizing and addressing bullying can also help maintain the integrity of these safe spaces. Support groups or clubs, such as Gender-Sexuality Alliances (GSAs), play a pivotal role. These groups provide a forum for students to discuss issues related to sexuality and gender identity in a supportive setting, which can be a powerful antidote to feelings of isolation and misunderstanding.

The Role of Educators and Staff in Safe Spaces

Educators and staff are the backbone of adequate, safe spaces. Their role is not just administrative but deeply personal. They act as facilitators, allies, and protectors within these spaces. They require specific training beyond general professional development to perform these roles effectively. This training should cover topics like LGBTQ+ terminology, the particular challenges faced by LGBTQ+ students, and the best practices for fostering an inclusive and supportive classroom environment.

Conflict resolution is another critical area in which educators and staff must be skilled. Conflicts can arise even in safe spaces, possibly related to misunderstandings, ingrained prejudices, or even resistance to the concept of safe spaces themselves. Staff should be prepared to handle these situations with sensitivity and assertiveness, ensuring that the safe space remains a sanctuary for all students. This might involve mediation skills, an understanding of restorative justice practices, and the ability to facilitate difficult conversations effectively.

Monitoring and Evaluating Safe Spaces

Safe spaces require ongoing monitoring and evaluation to remain effective. This process involves regularly assessing how these spaces function and their impact on students. Surveys and feedback forms can be valuable tools for gathering student input about their experiences in safe spaces. This feedback should gauge their sense of safety and inclusion and capture suggestions for improvement.

Evaluation should also consider broader indicators such as changes in school culture, shifts in attendance and academic performance among LGBTQ+ students, and the frequency of bullying incidents. These metrics can provide a more comprehensive view of the impact of safe spaces. Furthermore, regular review meetings involving staff, students, and possibly parents can help ensure that the safe spaces evolve to meet the changing needs of students and reflect new understandings and practices regarding LGBTQ+ issues.

Fostering safe spaces within educational settings is more than just providing a sanctuary. We're actively participating in transforming school cultures, making them more inclusive and supportive environments where every student can thrive. This proactive approach not only benefits LGBTQ+ students but enriches the entire educational community by promoting values of respect, inclusiveness, and mutual support.

Addressing Bullying and Discrimination in Schools

Bullying and discrimination within school walls are not just problems that disrupt student harmony; they are pervasive issues that deeply affect the mental health and academic performance of LGBTQ+ students. Imagine walking into school every day with the fear of being teased, isolated, or harassed simply for being who you are. This is a daily reality for many LGBTQ+ students across the globe. Statistics from various studies underscore the prevalence of such discrimination, revealing that a significant number of LGBTQ+ students face bullying behaviors that range from verbal harassment to physical violence. The effects of these experiences are profound, often leading to increased rates of depression, anxiety, and even thoughts of suicide, alongside a noticeable decline in academic engagement and performance.

The need for strong anti-bullying policies that explicitly address LGBTQ+ issues is critical in combating these detrimental effects. Schools must implement comprehensive policies that not only prohibit discrimination based on sexual orientation and gender identity but also provide clear consequences for those who engage in such behaviors. However, more than the presence of these policies on paper is needed. Enforcement is key. It involves effectively training teachers and administrators on recognizing and reacting to bullying incidents. Regular policy reviews are also required to ensure they adapt to new challenges and effectively protect students. Through firm policy enforcement, schools can create an environment where all students, regardless of their sexual orientation or gender identity, feel safe and valued.

Empowering LGBTQ+ students and their allies to stand against bullying is another crucial step in transforming school culture. Empowerment can take many forms, from forming student-led initiatives that promote inclusivity to establishing support groups where LGBTQ+ students and allies can share experiences and strategies. These groups often serve as a powerful platform for students to voice their concerns and advocate for changes within their schools. Moreover, involving students in creating educational campaigns can raise awareness about the issues LGBTQ+ students face and educate their peers on the importance of inclusivity and respect. When students lead by example, advocating for acceptance and challenging discriminatory behaviors, they empower themselves and pave the way for a more inclusive school environment for future generations.

Introducing restorative justice practices provides a compassionate and effective approach to resolving incidents of bullying and discrimination. Unlike traditional disciplinary actions, restorative justice focuses on the harm caused by the bullying behavior and seeks to repair that harm through inclusive and mediated dialogues. This approach brings together the victim, the perpetrator, and often a cross-section of the school community to discuss the impact of the bullying and work together to find a resolution that fosters healing and understanding. Through this process, perpetrators can understand the consequences of their actions and learn from their mistakes, while victims are provided a platform to express their feelings and needs. Restorative practices address the immediate bullying issues and promote long-term educational outcomes by improving relationships, reducing repeat offenses, and enhancing the school climate.

Embracing these strategies creates a multi-faceted approach to combatting bullying and discrimination centered on policy, empowerment, and restoration. By implementing and enforcing strong anti-bullying policies, empowering students to be advocates for change, and adopting restorative practices, schools can significantly reduce the incidence of bullying against LGBTQ+ students and create a more inclusive, supportive educational environment where every student has the opportunity to thrive without fear.

Building Inclusive Workplaces: A Guide for Employers

Creating a workplace that welcomes and actively supports LGBTQ+ employees requires more than just goodwill; it demands a structured approach to inclusivity that permeates every level of an organization. One fundamental step is the adoption of inclusive employment policies. These policies should explicitly prohibit discrimination based on sexual orientation and gender identity. But inclusion goes beyond non-discrimination. It involves crafting policies that address the specific needs of LGBTQ+ employees, such as inclusive health benefits that cover partners of all genders and support for transgender employees in accessing gender-affirming healthcare. Furthermore, policies should acknowledge and facilitate name changes and gender updates in company records without burdening the employee.

To breathe life into these policies, companies must ensure that they are not just words on a page but are understood, respected, and enforced across the organization. This starts with comprehensive diversity and inclusion training sessions for all employees. Such training should cover the basics of LGBTQ+ identity and inclusion, delve into specific issues like unconscious bias and microaggressions, and equip employees with practical skills to create an inclusive environment. These sessions should not be a one-time event but part of an ongoing educational effort that helps build a genuinely inclusive corporate culture.

Alongside policy and training, another powerful tool in fostering an inclusive workplace is forming LGBTQ+ employee resource groups (ERGs). These groups provide a space for LGBTQ+ employees and allies to come together, share experiences, and discuss issues relevant to the community. ERGs can also play a crucial advocacy role within the company, advising on and helping to implement inclusive policies and practices. The presence of an active ERG can be a clear signal of a company's commitment to diversity and inclusion, making it not just a more attractive place for LGBTQ+ individuals to work but also enhancing the organization's reputation externally.

Regular workplace culture assessments are essential to ensure that inclusion efforts are implemented and effective. These evaluations should look at various indicators of an inclusive environment, such as employee satisfaction, retention rates of LGBTQ+ employees, and feedback from inclusion training sessions. Surveys can be a useful tool here, providing insights into the experiences and perceptions of employees regarding the company's inclusivity. The results can help identify areas where the company is succeeding and areas where further work is needed, ensuring that efforts to create a welcoming workplace for LGBTQ+ employees are continuously refined and improved.

By implementing clear policies, comprehensive training, active ERGs, and regular cultural assessments, employers can create work environments where LGBTQ+ employees feel truly valued and supported. This benefits the individuals involved and enhances the overall productivity and morale of the entire workforce. In today's increasingly diverse and connected world, such inclusivity can be a significant asset, attracting top talent and fostering innovation and collaboration across the company. As employers, embracing this challenge is not just the right thing to do; it's a smart business strategy that pays dividends in employee engagement, retention, and corporate reputation.

Navigating Gender Identity in Professional Settings

Navigating gender identity at work can be challenging. It's about staying true to yourself while fitting into professional norms. Clear, supportive policies around gender identity help everyone feel confident and respected. This includes having rules for pronoun usage, gender-neutral facilities, and dress codes. It's not just about following the rules—it's about recognizing and affirming everyone's identity.

For instance, clear guidelines on pronoun usage can be set through simple practices such as adding pronouns to email signatures, which promotes a culture of respect and recognition. It's a small, almost effortless act, yet it can significantly impact someone's experience at work, ensuring they feel seen and respected. Similarly, implementing gender-neutral facilities, like restrooms and changing rooms, removes unnecessary stress for transgender and nonbinary employees, who might otherwise face discomfort or anxiety over something as basic as using the restroom at work. Dress codes, too, need a thoughtful overhaul to ensure they are inclusive and flexible, avoiding rigid gender norms that do not accommodate the spectrum of gender identities.

Supporting employees through gender transition is perhaps one of the most tangible ways a workplace can express its commitment to inclusivity. This support can manifest in various forms, from transparent communication policies that respect an employee's privacy to more tangible support mechanisms like providing adequate medical leave for those undergoing transition-related procedures. These policies must be communicated clearly and early in an employee's transition journey. For example, HR departments can develop transition guidelines that outline everything from the procedural aspects of transitioning at work (like name changes in official records) to the support systems in place, such as counseling or medical leave policies. This not only aids the transitioning employee but also educates the entire workforce on the process, fostering an environment of understanding and support.

Creating an affirmative environment goes beyond policy—nurturing a culture where all employees feel they can thrive. This includes training sessions that educate employees about gender identity and its nuances, which can help prevent misgendering and promote a more inclusive atmosphere. Regular workshops and seminars can keep this education ongoing, addressing new issues and refreshing older information, ensuring that inclusivity remains a living, evolving part of the company culture.

Case studies from various organizations highlight the success of these practices. For example, a tech company in Silicon Valley implemented a comprehensive program for supporting transitioning employees, which included everything from medical leave to psychological support and gender-sensitivity training for their teams. The result was a smoother transition for the employees involved and a more aware and cohesive team dynamic that appreciated the courage and authenticity of its members. Another case from a multinational corporation involved updating their global HR policies to include gender identity clauses, which standardized supportive practices across all their locations, ensuring that employees received equal support and recognition, irrespective of geographical location.

Navigating gender identity professionally isn't just about adhering to legal requirements or following trends. It's about recognizing and celebrating the diverse identities that employees bring to their professional spaces. By implementing thoughtful policies, providing robust support systems, and fostering an environment of continuous learning and respect, companies can turn the challenge of navigating gender identity into an opportunity for growth, innovation, and unity. This commitment not only enhances the work experience for

LGBTQ+ employees but also enriches the entire company by creating a more inclusive, empathetic, and diverse workplace.

Allyship in Action: Effective Support from Non-LGBTQ+ Colleagues

Allyship in the workplace and educational settings means more than just supporting diversity initiatives on paper; it's about non-LGBTQ+ individuals actively participating in creating environments where everyone, irrespective of their gender identity or sexual orientation, feels valued and supported. True allies are those who understand their role in challenging heteronormative assumptions and advocating for inclusive practices that uplift their LGBTQ+ colleagues and classmates.

Defining Effective Allyship

Being an ally involves a commitment to ongoing education about LGBTQ+ issues and using one's position of privilege to advocate for change. It means standing up against discrimination, not just when it's convenient, but every time you see it, ensuring that your LGBTQ+ peers can thrive in a supportive environment. True allyship requires action—it's about doing the work to ensure inclusivity is sewn into the fabric of the workplace and educational institutions.

Practical Steps for Allies

For allies, the journey towards effective support starts with education. Familiarize yourself with the basic concepts related to LGBTQ+ identities, including the correct usage of pronouns and understanding different sexual orientations and gender expressions. This foundational knowledge is crucial in helping you navigate interactions respectfully and thoughtfully.

Beyond personal education, advocate for policies and practices that support inclusivity. This could involve lobbying for the implementation of comprehensive non-discrimination policies, supporting the creation of gender-neutral facilities, or ensuring that health benefits are inclusive of LGBTQ+ needs. Participation in diversity and inclusion training sessions broadens your understanding and equips you with the tools to help effect change. Furthermore, allies can support—or even help organize—events like Pride celebrations or workshops focused on LGBTQ+ issues, contributing to a culture of openness and acceptance.

Challenges Allies May Face

Despite your best intentions, the allyship path can sometimes be challenged. Misunderstandings and misconceptions about what it means to be an ally can arise. For instance, some might believe that allyship is an invasion of space or an attempt to speak over the LGBTQ+ community. It's crucial to approach allyship with humility, always ready to listen more than you talk and to step back when necessary. The role of an ally is not to lead the conversation but to support and amplify the voices of LGBTQ+ individuals.

Another common challenge is the fear of saying or doing the wrong thing. This fear can be paralyzing, but it's important to remember that making mistakes is a part of learning and growing. What matters most is your willingness to learn from these mistakes and to continue showing up and standing up for what's right.

Celebrating Ally Successes

There are countless stories of allies impacting their workplaces and schools. For example, consider a team leader who successfully advocated for transgender-inclusive health benefits at their company, significantly easing the burden for transgender employees undergoing transition-related care. Or a teacher who organized an after-school program to educate students on LGBTQ+ history, fostering a deeper understanding and respect among students.

These stories celebrate the successes and serve as powerful reminders of effective allyship's impact. They inspire others to take action and show that change is possible, encouraging a ripple effect of allyship that can transform entire communities.

In embracing the role of an ally, you contribute to a culture where inclusivity isn't just an ideal but a lived reality. This chapter not only outlines the steps you can take to support your LGBTQ+ colleagues and classmates but also highlights the profound impact such support can have on individuals and institutions alike. As we turn the page to the next chapter, let's carry forward the commitment to act, advocate, and ally, knowing that our collective efforts are crucial in shaping a more inclusive, respectful, and uplifting environment for everyone.

SEVEN

Community Support and Resources

In a world that often feels like it's spinning too fast, finding your tribe and your community can sometimes seem like searching for a signal in a storm. For LGBTQ+ individuals, the quest for connection and support carries an added layer of urgency. The collective journey of self-discovery, acceptance, and advocacy isn't just about personal growth—it's about survival and resilience in the face of adversities that many cannot fathom. This chapter explores the robust networks and innovative platforms that offer sanctuary and empower you to raise your voice, amplify your impact, and shield your privacy in a world where you are still learning to embrace diversity fully.

Leveraging Online Platforms for Support and Activism

Explore Digital Communities

The digital era has ushered in unprecedented opportunities for community building and support. Online platforms have become pivotal in connecting LGBTQ+ individuals across the globe, breaking down geographical and societal barriers that once isolated us. Forums like Reddit and specialized LGBTQ+ websites serve as bustling digital crossroads where you can share experiences, seek advice, and find camaraderie. Social media groups like Facebook and Instagram offer spaces where identities are celebrated through vibrant storytelling and visual expression. These communities, each unique in their ambiance and focus, provide vital connections that can transform a solitary struggle into a shared narrative.

Navigating these platforms, you'll find that each serves a different purpose. Some may be more discussion-oriented, perfect for seeking guidance or understanding complex issues surrounding gender and sexuality. Others might focus on activism, providing updates on LGBTQ+ rights and opportunities to engage in digital advocacy efforts. Then there are support-oriented groups, where conversations often delve into personal challenges and triumphs, offering a mirror to your own experiences and feelings. Engaging with these communities, you absorb not just the knowledge and stories shared but also gain a sense of belonging and validation that the physical spaces around you may not provide.

Guide to Online Activism

Digital platforms are not just about support; they are powerful tools for activism. Online activism allows you to participate in global movements from your living room, contributing to causes that matter deeply to you. The key to effective online activism lies in understanding how to use digital tools to your advantage—whether it's through organizing virtual events, participating in hashtag campaigns, or spreading awareness through shareable content.

For instance, consider the impact of global hashtag campaigns like #LoveWins or #TransRightsAreHumanRights. These movements started small but grew into global phenomena, significantly influencing public opinion and policy. By joining these campaigns, you contribute to a larger narrative that seeks to shift cultural and legal landscapes worldwide. Moreover, online platforms can help coordinate local events, rallies, or fundraisers, amplifying your impact in tangible ways that resonate within and beyond your community.

Ensuring Online Safety

While the digital world opens up incredible avenues for connection and activism, it also requires vigilance to navigate safely, especially in regions where LGBTQ+ rights are under threat. Protecting your privacy online is crucial. Start by familiarizing yourself with the privacy settings on each platform you use. Be cautious about the personal information you share online, and consider using pseudonyms or anonymous profiles when discussing sensitive topics.

It's also wise to be aware of the digital footprint you leave. Regularly reviewing your shared content and connections can help prevent unintended exposure to your personal life, especially in professional or familial settings that may not be welcoming. Encrypted messaging apps for private conversations can add an extra layer of security, ensuring your communications on sensitive matters remain confidential.

Examples of Impactful Online Movements

Reflecting on successful online movements provides inspiration and valuable lessons on the power of digital solidarity. Take the example of the "It Gets Better" project, which started as a simple online video campaign to provide hope and support to LGBTQ+ youth facing harassment. This movement rapidly grew into a global phenomenon, significantly impacting the lives of countless individuals by offering them stories of resilience and a promise of a better future.

Another impactful campaign, #NoH8, utilized visual media to protest against legislation banning same-sex marriage. Participants in the campaign included high-profile celebrities and everyday citizens, who posted photos with "NOH8" painted on their faces, creating a powerful visual statement that echoed across social media platforms, influencing public opinion and policy discussions.

These examples underscore the transformative potential of online platforms in driving social change. By participating in or even initiating online movements, you harness the collective power of the digital community to advocate for equality, justice, and acceptance—no matter where you are in the world.

In a space where every click can connect, inform, or inspire, the digital world offers tools for finding and building your community. As you navigate these platforms, remember that each interaction, share, and hashtag is a ripple in the broader narrative of the LGBTQ+ experience. This narrative grows richer and more resonant with every voice that joins in.

Local and National LGBTQ+ Support Organizations

In the vast landscape of support that cradles our LGBTQ+ community, local and national organizations stand as pillars of strength and refuge. These organizations stitch together a network of resources from coast to coast, offering everything from legal aid and mental health counseling to educational workshops and housing assistance. They are support providers, life changers, community builders, and safe havens.

Directory of Organizations

Imagine a map, each pin representing an organization dedicated to serving the LGBTQ+ community uniquely. These organizations vary widely in their focus and the breadth of services they offer. For instance, The Trevor Project operates nationally, offering crisis intervention and suicide prevention services specifically targeted at LGBTQ+ youth. Their 24/7 hotline is a lifeline for many, providing immediate access to support when it's most needed. On a more localized level, organizations like the San Francisco LGBT Center offer a range of services, including career counseling and rental assistance, all tailored to meet the specific needs of their community members.

Each organization, whether operating on a large scale or within a local community, plays a crucial role in the ecosystem of LGBTQ+ support. Their services are designed to meet immediate needs and foster long-term resilience and empowerment within the community. To facilitate access to these vital resources, many organizations are listed in online directories such as CenterLink, which provides a searchable database of LGBTQ+ community centers across the United

States and worldwide. These directories often include detailed information about the services offered by each organization, contact information, and how to access their resources.

Engaging with Organizations

Engagement with these organizations can take many forms, depending on your interests and needs. Volunteering is a powerful way to give back, offering your skills and time to support their missions. This might involve helping at events, providing administrative support, or lending your professional marketing or legal services expertise. For those seeking support, these organizations often offer counseling, support groups, and educational programs that can provide crucial guidance and community connection. Participating in these programs can be a transformative experience, offering support and opportunities for personal growth and community building.

Moreover, many organizations host events and workshops that can be pivotal in expanding your understanding of LGBTQ+ issues and advocacy strategies. These events serve as educational opportunities and community-building spaces where you can meet others who share your experiences and commitments. By engaging with these organizations, you access numerous resources and become part of a broader community effort to uplift and support LGBTQ+ individuals.

Spotlight on Diverse Services

The range of services provided by LGBTQ+ organizations is as diverse as the community itself. Legal organizations like Lambda Legal offer legal representation and advocacy to advance the civil rights of LGBTQ+ people, ensuring justice and equality under the law. Mental health services provided by organizations such as GLMA: Health Professionals Advancing LGBTQ Equality focus on promoting the health and well-being of LGBTQ+ individuals through advocacy, education, and providing culturally competent medical services.

In addition to advocacy and health services, many organizations offer educational programs to inform and empower. These programs cover a wide range of topics, from safe sex education to rights awareness, equipping participants with the knowledge needed to navigate their lives confidently and safely. Housing assistance is another critical service provided by organizations like the Ali Forney Center in New York City, which specializes in helping homeless LGBTQ+ youth secure stable and safe housing, a vital component of personal security and well-being.

Case Studies of Successful Interventions

The impact of these organizations can be seen in countless individual stories of transformation and support. For example, a young transgender woman found refuge and support at a local LGBTQ+ center after being ostracized by her family. Through the center's counseling services and support groups, she rebuilt her confidence, pursued gender-affirming care, and eventually became a volunteer at the center, helping others facing similar challenges. Another case involves a nationwide campaign organized by a prominent LGBTQ+ legal organization that successfully challenged discriminatory laws and practices, leading to significant legal victories that benefited countless community members.

These case studies not only highlight the critical role played by LGBTQ+ support organizations but also underscore the tangible, life-changing impact of their services. Through their comprehensive and diverse offerings, these organizations address immediate needs and pave the way for a more inclusive and equitable society. By connecting with these organizations as a volunteer, participant or advocate, you become an integral part of a dynamic network that supports and empowers the LGBTQ+ community at every level.

Mental Health Hotlines and How They Can Help

Sometimes, having someone to talk to can be a crucial lifeline when dealing with mental health challenges. For many in the LGBTQ+ community who might feel isolated or misunderstood in their immediate environments, mental health hotlines offer a confidential, accessible form of support that can be crucial in times of crisis or distress. These hotlines are staffed by individuals who understand the unique challenges faced by LGBTQ+ individuals, making them an invaluable resource in fostering emotional resilience and immediate access to help.

List of Hotlines

A myriad of national and international hotlines, tailored specifically to serve the LGBTQ+ community, offering support in multiple languages and across various time zones. For instance, services like The Trevor Project provide 24/7 crisis intervention and suicide prevention services specifically for LGBTQ+ youth. Meanwhile, Trans Lifeline offers dedicated support for transgender individuals, staffed by people who are themselves transgender, ensuring a deep, personal understanding of the callers' experiences. Other notable hotlines include the GLBT National Help Center, which provides peer support, community connections, and resource information. Each hotline is designed to meet you where you are, offering a spectrum of support from emotional counseling to guidance on navigating mental health systems.

Benefits of Hotlines

The advantages of utilizing these hotlines are manifold. Anonymity is one of the most significant benefits, providing a safe space to express your feelings and concerns without fear of judgment or exposure. This can be especially important if you're not yet out about your sexual orientation or gender identity or if you're in an environment that is not supportive. Immediate access to support is another critical benefit. A crisis doesn't have a schedule; it can strike at any moment, and having a hotline at your fingertips means you're only a phone call away from professional support. Furthermore, these hotlines often act as a first line of defense in crisis intervention, offering immediate strategies to manage acute emotional distress and, if necessary, referring callers to emergency services or longer-term treatment solutions.

How to Use Hotlines Effectively

It's helpful to understand how best to communicate your needs during a call to make the most of these services. Preparing a summary of your situation and feelings can help you articulate your thoughts more clearly, especially in severe distress. It's also useful to have a list of questions you might want to ask, such as inquiries about additional resources, follow-up support, or recommendations for therapists experienced in dealing with LGBTQ+ issues. Remember, the person on the other end of the line is there to support you, so try to be as open as you feel comfortable being. This will help them provide the most accurate and supportive guidance tailored to your situation.

Testimonials

Countless testimonials highlight the impact of these hotlines, with many individuals finding hope and support through their services. One anonymous user shared, "Calling the hotline was a turning point for me. I felt so alone and overwhelmed, but the person on the other end of the line listened without judgment. They helped me see that I wasn't alone and that there were steps I could take to feel better. It was a conversation that saved my life." Another mentioned, "It was the middle of the night, and I felt like I couldn't talk to anyone. The volunteer who answered my call helped calm me down and gave me the courage to seek further help. I'm so grateful for that."

These voices underscore the profound role that mental health hotlines can play in the lives of LGBTQ+ individuals. They offer immediate relief and safety in moments of crisis and connect callers to a wider community and ongoing support, reinforcing the message that no one has to navigate their mental health journey alone. As you consider the resources available, remember these hotlines are there, ready to listen and help at any hour of the day, providing a confidential and compassionate lifeline whenever you need it.

Community Centers: A Hub for Connection and Support

Imagine walking into a space where every wall, every face, every program speaks to the essence of who you are and who you aspire to be. This is the heart of what the LGBTQ+ community centers worldwide strive to provide—a sanctuary where acceptance is the norm and support is given. These centers are not just physical structures; they are vibrant hubs of activity and support, pulsating with the collective energy of the community they serve. They serve as sources of hope and strength in the LGBTQ+ community, offering essential services such as health care, counseling, educational workshops, and cultural celebrations.

The journey can often start with a simple internet search for a community center. Most major cities and even smaller towns increasingly have centers, each offering a range of programs and resources tailored to the needs of their local LGBTQ+ population. Websites like CenterLink (lgbtcenters.org) offer a comprehensive directory of LGBTQ+ community centers worldwide, making locating a center near you easier. Once you find a center, visiting it can be an enlightening experience. Expect to be greeted with open arms, as these centers are designed to be welcoming spaces for all, regardless of where you are in your journey. From the moment you step in, you'll find bulletin boards bursting with flyers for upcoming events, friendly faces eager to explain their services, and an atmosphere filled with the chatter of community members connecting and sharing.

The array of programs and services offered at these community centers is as diverse as the community. Health services often include HIV testing and counseling, mental health support groups, and, in some cases, clinics that provide hormone replacement therapy (HRT) or other medical services specifically for transgender clients. Career counseling services might help with resume building, job searches, or even dressing for success. Moreover, many centers offer educational workshops that cover a broad range of topics, from legal rights and advocacy to health and wellness. Cultural events, such as movie nights, art shows, and poetry readings, celebrate the rich diversity of the LGBTQ+

community, providing a space for learning, joy and celebration.

The stories of transformation and community within these centers' walls are profound and uplifting. Take, for example, Malcolm, who stumbled into a community center on the brink of homelessness. The center not only provided emergency housing resources but also connected him with counseling services to support his mental health. Over time, Malcolm went from receiving support to giving it, eventually leading community workshops on LGBTQ+ rights. Then there's Devon, who attended a coding workshop at her local LGBTQ+ community center, which sparked a career transition into tech. These centers gave Malcolm and Devon the needed resources and a community that saw and supported them at every step.

Community centers operate on the fundamental belief that everyone should have access to the resources and support they need to live fully and freely. They are more than just safe spaces —they launch pads for empowerment and catalysts for personal and collective growth. In these spaces, connections are made, movements are born, and lives are transformed, all within the embrace of a community that understands the unique joys and challenges of the LGBTQ+ experience. As you consider visiting or engaging with a community center, know that what you'll find there has the potential to support you and inspire and transform you in ways that resonate far beyond the center's walls.

Creating Virtual Safe Spaces for Marginalized Groups

In the vast expanse of the internet, finding a corner where you can truly be yourself, free from judgment or harm, is invaluable.

Virtual safe spaces are crucial for marginalized groups within the LGBTQ+ community—spaces where transgender youth, queer people of color, and those living in less accepting regions can gather, share, and support each other safely. These spaces are not just about social interaction; they are sanctuaries that provide comfort, advice, and a sense of community that might be lacking in physical environments that are hostile or indifferent to LGBTQ+ identities.

Creating these virtual safe spaces requires careful consideration and planning to ensure they truly serve the needs of their members. Choosing the right platform is the first step. While mainstream social media platforms can be useful, they often come with risks of exposure to larger, potentially hostile audiences. Private platforms like Discord or Slack, which offer controlled access and robust moderation tools, can be more suitable. These platforms allow you to create invite-only groups where members can interact in a controlled and secure environment, away from the prying eyes of the outside world.

Once the platform is chosen, establishing ground rules is essential. These rules should be clear and enforceable, designed to create an environment of respect and safety. They might include guidelines on confidentiality, the kinds of language that are acceptable, and how members can interact with each other. All members must agree to these rules before joining, ensuring everyone is committed to maintaining a safe space. Moderators play a crucial role here, not just in enforcing the rules but in setting the tone of the community, being approachable, and acting swiftly and sensitively to resolve any issues that arise.

Promoting inclusivity is another critical aspect. This means going beyond just setting up the space and waiting for people to come. Active outreach is important, especially to those who feel isolated or vulnerable. This could involve collaborating with other LGBTQ+ organizations that can help spread the word or using social media to reach a wider audience while carefully managing privacy and security. Inclusivity also means ensuring the space meets the diverse needs of its members, accommodating differences in language, cultural background, and accessibility.

Examples of successful virtual safe spaces abound, offering insights into how these communities can thrive. One notable example is a virtual support group set up for transgender teenagers, which uses a secure, invitation-only forum to discuss everything from gender identity to mental health. The group not only provides emotional support but also shares resources like information on local healthcare providers that offer transgender-friendly services. Another example is a virtual community for queer people of color that organizes regular video chats and webinars, creating a platform for members to connect, learn, and empower each other, bridging the gap between geographical distances.

These examples highlight the transformative power of virtual safe spaces. They show how, with the right tools and intentions, the digital world can offer real-world sanctuaries for those who might otherwise feel isolated or endangered. By fostering these spaces, we provide essential support and connection and empower members of the LGBTQ+ community to navigate their lives with greater confidence and security. As you consider engaging with or creating a virtual safe space, remember the profound impact such a community can have—not just in providing a refuge from the world's adversities but in building bridges that connect us all in our shared human experience.

Resource Lists for Ongoing Learning and Support

In the vast ocean of information we navigate daily, having curated lists of resources specifically tailored for the LGBTQ+ community can be like finding a lighthouse guiding us to a safe harbor. These resources, ranging from insightful books and articles to enlightening podcasts and videos, inform, empower and connect us. As someone deeply committed to your growth and empowerment, I understand the importance of providing these resources and ensuring they are accessible, relevant, and continually updated to reflect the latest insights and advancements.

Curated Resource Lists

Imagine having a toolkit at your fingertips, one that includes an array of carefully selected books like *"The Queer Advantage"* by Andrew Gelwicks, which celebrates the unique and compelling perspectives that LGBTQ+ individuals bring to the world. Add a collection of articles from platforms like *Them* and *Out*, which provide contemporary analyses and feature stories that resonate with your experiences. Podcasts like *Nancy* from WNYC Studios weave stories touching on issues from identity politics to cultural discussions, offering solace and inspiration through your headphones. Videos, perhaps a series like *"Queer Eye,"* not only entertain but also deepen our understanding of the diverse lives within our community, promoting a broader acceptance and celebration of our differences.

Accessibility of these resources is paramount. It ensures that everyone, regardless of educational background or first language, can benefit from the knowledge and support available. This means selecting resources available in multiple formats—be it audio, visual, or written—that are easy to understand. It also involves choosing free or low-cost resources to ensure financial barriers do not hinder access. Libraries, community centers, and online platforms often offer these resources for free, providing easy access to anyone with an internet connection.

Updating Resource Lists

The landscape of LGBTQ+ rights, culture, and understanding is constantly evolving. What was groundbreaking a few years ago may be outdated, and new challenges and milestones continually reshape our community's needs and narratives. Therefore, maintaining up-to-date resource lists is crucial. This might involve annual reviews of the materials recommended, checking for any new research, significant cultural shifts, or technological advancements that could impact the relevance and effectiveness of the resources provided. Engaging with community feedback is also vital in this process. Insights from users like you help assess the impact of the resources and identify gaps that new materials could fill.

Encouraging Self-Education

The power of self-education cannot be overstated. It's about taking ownership of your personal and community growth, actively seeking out knowledge, and engaging with materials that challenge and inspire you. This proactive approach to learning fosters a deeper personal connection to the material, enhancing its immediate relevance and long-term impact on your life. Encouraging this involves providing resources and creating an environment that supports and motivates continuous learning. This could be through discussion groups, both online and offline, where you and your peers discuss and debate topics covered in your readings or viewings. It could also involve interactive elements like quizzes or projects that allow you to apply what you've learned in practical, impactful ways.

These resources keep you informed and actively participate in broader cultural and communal dialogue. You are equipping yourself with the tools to navigate your identity and relationships, advocate for your rights, and contribute to the ongoing fight for equality and understanding. Remember, every article read, podcast, and video watched is a step towards a more informed, empowered, and empathetic life.

In wrapping up this exploration of community support and resources, we've navigated through the digital and physical spaces that house our collective hopes, struggles, and triumphs. Each resource and space offers unique avenues for connection, learning, and activism, from the dynamic realms of online platforms to the foundational support of local and national organizations. As we transition from this chapter, remember that the journey of self-discovery and community building is ongoing—a continuous process of learning, supporting, and growing together. Let's commit to harnessing these resources and insights, paving the way toward a future where everyone can thrive in authenticity and freedom.

EIGHT

Personal Narratives and Empowerment

Imagine you're holding a mosaic, each piece a story of struggle, triumph, and unwavering resilience. This chapter is that mosaic for the LGBTQ+ community, a collection of powerful narratives that illuminate the pathways through mental health challenges, each tile a testament to the strength found in vulnerability and support. Here, we explore the lives of individuals who have faced significant mental health challenges and emerged stronger. They have turned their darkest moments into sources of hope for others.

Stories of Resilience: Overcoming Mental Health Challenges

In a world that often feels like it's built for someone else, the stories of Leo, Katrina, and Priya stand out as testaments to the power of resilience and the profound impact of supportive communities and professional help. These narratives are not just stories but lifelines for those who might see parts of their journey mirrored in these experiences.

Leo, a transgender man of color, faced what seemed like insurmountable obstacles from a young age. Bullied for his gender nonconformity and estranged from unsupportive family members, Leo's mental health teetered on the brink of despair. Yet, his story took a turn when he connected with a local LGBTQ+ youth group and found allies and champions in his corner. This community, coupled with therapy that respected and affirmed his identity, gave Leo the tools to rebuild his self-worth. Today, Leo uses his journey to inspire others as a speaker and advocate, focusing on the importance of mental health support for transgender youth.

Katrina's narrative unfolds differently but is equally impactful. A bisexual woman battling severe depression, Katrina felt isolated by the invisibility she experienced within both straight and gay communities. Her breakthrough came through an LGBTQ+ inclusive therapy group where she could express her fears and frustrations without judgment. This environment, where her bisexuality was neither questioned nor dismissed, was pivotal. It was here that Katrina learned coping strategies that acknowledged the unique challenges of her bisexual identity, helping her to navigate her mental health with a newfound confidence.

Priya, a genderqueer immigrant, brings another layer to our mosaic. Facing cultural stigmatization both within and outside LGBTQ+ spaces, Priya struggled to find a therapist who understood the intersectionality of their identity. Persistence led them to an online therapy service specializing in LGBTQ+ and immigrant mental health. This transformative service offered Priya therapy and a gateway to understanding and integrating their complex identities. Now, Priya volunteers for the same service, guiding others toward healing and self-acceptance.

Each story is distinct, yet all echo a common theme: the transformative role of therapy and support systems. Leo, Katrina, and Priya's experiences highlight how tailored mental health care and community support can catalyze recovery and empowerment. Their journeys offer hope and actionable insights for those facing similar struggles, illustrating that overcoming mental health challenges is possible and an avenue to empowering others with the proper support.

Reflection Section

Consider this: What would it look like if you placed your own story within this mosaic? How has your unique journey shaped your view on mental health, and what strategies have helped you? Reflecting on these questions can be a powerful exercise in understanding your path and recognizing the strength in your story.

These narratives are more than just accounts of personal hardship and recovery; they are a call to action for all of us to support and uplift each other. In sharing these stories, we foster a deeper understanding of the diverse challenges within our community and strengthen our collective commitment to advocating for mental health resources that are inclusive and affirming of all identities. As you turn these pages, let the resilience of Leo, Katrina, and Priya inspire you to advocate for yourself and others, reinforcing the belief that every individual deserves the chance to write their own story of recovery and empowerment.

Transition Journeys: Insights and Inspirations

Transgender and nonbinary individuals have unique and powerful stories of courage, discovery, and transformation. Each person's journey adds to the rich diversity of human experiences, showcasing their vibrant and revealing lives. This section combines a diverse collection of transition stories, providing an overview of personal journeys that include social, medical, and legal changes. Each narrative highlights personal victories and challenges and sheds light on the profound impact of transitioning on one's identity and well-being.

Consider the story of Blake, a nonbinary person who navigated the complex terrain of social transition in a small, conservative town. The social aspect of Blake's transition involved coming out to family, friends, and colleagues—a process met with mixed reactions that ranged from supportive to dismissive. The lack of local support groups and visible LGBTQ+ community members compounded Blake's challenges. However, victory came through finding solidarity online and establishing a supportive network transcending geographical boundaries. Blake's journey underscores the importance of virtual and physical community in reinforcing one's sense of identity and belonging during transition.

On the medical front, Reagan's transition story encapsulates the hurdles and triumphs associated with accessing gender-affirming healthcare. Starting hormone replacement therapy (HRT) was a pivotal moment for Reagan, one that brought immense joy but also significant challenges, including navigating the healthcare system, dealing with insurance hurdles, and managing the physical and emotional effects of hormonal changes. Reagan's perseverance through these obstacles was facilitated by knowledgeable healthcare providers who offered medical support and validated Reagan's identity, significantly enhancing Reagan's overall well-being.

Legally, Ethan's transition journey highlights the challenges of updating personal identification documents to reflect one's true gender. The process, fraught with bureaucratic red tape and varying requirements from state to state, tested Ethan's resilience. Success came through persistence and the assistance of a legal advocacy group specializing in LGBTQ+ rights, which guided Ethan through the legal complexities. The moment Ethan received a driver's license that accurately reflected their gender was more than a legal victory—it was a profound affirmation of their identity.

These stories, diverse in their paths and outcomes, offer invaluable insights for those contemplating or undergoing similar journeys. From Blake, we learn the power of finding community support; from Reagan, we learn the importance of advocating for one's health needs; and from Ethan, we learn the importance of legal recognition in affirming one's identity. For readers navigating their transitions, these narratives provide a roadmap and a reminder of the resilience and triumph possible on this path.

Interactive Element: Transition Planning Worksheet

To further assist you in your transition journey, consider using a Transition Planning Worksheet. This tool can help you organize your goals, track progress, and manage your transition's logistical and emotional aspects. The worksheet could include sections for medical care planning, legal document updates, and social transition steps, providing a structured way to approach what can often feel overwhelming. This resource aims to empower you to take control of your transition, ensuring that each step is thoughtfully considered and aligned with your overall well-being.

Activism on the Front Lines: Personal Accounts

In advocacy, it's the activists on the front lines of the LGBTQ+ movement who make the biggest impact. Their stories are narratives of personal commitment and powerful demonstrations of how passion can influence change and challenge societal norms. Consider the stories of Wyatt, Addison, and Asha, who have uniquely carved out spaces for empowerment and advocacy, confronting myriad challenges while catalyzing significant progress within the LGBTQ+ community.

A seasoned activist, Wyatt has been heavily involved in legal activism, focusing on transgender rights. Their journey began in a small community where transgender individuals faced significant legal discrimination. Motivated by personal experiences of injustice, Wyatt spearheaded initiatives to change discriminatory laws. This involved organizing rallies, engaging with lawmakers, and providing testimonies in court cases. The road was fraught with challenges, including substantial opposition from conservative groups and the emotional toll of high-stakes activism. However, Wyatt's efforts bore fruit when several laws were amended, granting better protections for transgender people in their state. This victory was more than a legal win; it was a source of hope for many and a testament to the power of persistent, informed advocacy.

Addison's activism paints a different picture, highlighting the power of educational outreach. As a bisexual person of color,

Addison felt compelled to address the lack of LGBTQ+ inclusivity in educational content. They launched a series of workshops in schools and colleges, focusing on LGBTQ+ history and rights. The initial pushback was disheartening—some institutions hesitated to include what they deemed 'sensitive topics' in their curriculum. However, Addison's persistence led to breakthroughs, with several educational institutions revising their curricula to include comprehensive LGBTQ+ content. These workshops taught students the understanding necessary to foster inclusivity within their communities. Addison's journey underscores the transformative impact of infusing education with activism, altering perceptions one workshop at a time.

Asha's story highlights the world of online activism, where advocacy and technology intersect. Recognizing the global reach of social media, Asha utilized these platforms to launch campaigns aimed at raising awareness about issues affecting queer individuals in conservative regions. Through viral campaigns, virtual protests, and collaborations with international LGBTQ+ organizations, Asha drew attention to pressing issues, rallying a global community of support and action. The challenge was immense, dealing with cyber-bullying and often intense scrutiny. Still, the solidarity and support from these campaigns fostered a sense of global community and collective resilience that transcended borders.

From these narratives, several lessons emerge for aspiring activists. First, the importance of resilience cannot be overstated—the path of advocacy is often strewn with obstacles, but persistence can lead to impactful change. Second, the power of community and collaboration plays a critical role in amplifying advocacy efforts; finding allies can provide the support and resources necessary to sustain campaigns. Lastly, adapting to the context of your activism—whether it involves direct legal challenges, educational initiatives, or digital campaigns—is crucial for effective advocacy.

As you reflect on these stories, consider how your voice and actions can contribute to the ongoing fight for LGBTQ+ rights. Whether you're inspired to initiate a local project, join an existing movement, or simply support advocacy efforts in your capacity, remember that every action contributes to a larger wave of change. By stepping into the activism arena, you join a community of courageous individuals who are not just dreaming of a better future but actively working towards it.

Lessons in Love and Acceptance: Family and Relationships

Family dynamics and personal relationships within the LGBTQ+ community can often be uncharted and unfamiliar, presenting unique challenges and experiences. Yet, amidst these complex interactions, profound stories of acceptance, resilience, and transformation resonate deeply with those seeking harmony in their connections. These stories shed light on the journey to familial acceptance and highlight the diverse relationships that form the foundation of the LGBTQ+ community's support network.

Take, for example, the story of Ella, a lesbian woman who grappled with coming out to her traditionally conservative family. The journey was fraught with fear and uncertainty, as Ella worried about losing the love and support of those closest to her. The turning point came during a family gathering, where, with trembling hands and a voice laced with emotion, she shared her truth. To her surprise, her revelation was met not with rejection but with an outpouring of love and acceptance from her younger sister, Lisa. Lisa's support was pivotal; she helped mediate conversations with other family members, explaining the importance of acceptance and challenging preconceived notions about sexuality. Over time, this open dialogue fostered a deeper understanding and acceptance within the family, transforming their relationships into sources of strength and affirmation for Ella.

In romantic partnerships and chosen families within the LGBTQ+ community, the dynamics are as diverse as the individuals involved. These relationships can take many forms, reflecting each person's unique identities and experiences. Consider the relationship between Jade and Elliott, a transgender man and a nonbinary individual, respectively, whose partnership is a testament to the power of mutual respect and understanding. Their relationship navigates the complexities of gender identity with openness and empathy, serving as a foundation for personal growth and collective resilience. Together, they have built a chosen family, a close-knit group of friends from various backgrounds, united by shared experiences and a common commitment to supporting one another. This chosen family gathers regularly, celebrating milestones and supporting each other through challenges, embodying the essence of community and belonging.

Rejection, unfortunately, remains a harsh reality for many in the LGBTQ+ community, and coping with it is an ordeal that tests the resilience of even the strongest individuals. Liam, a gay man, faced stark rejection from his parents, who could not come to terms with his sexuality. The pain of this rejection was profound, leaving him feeling isolated and misunderstood.

However, Liam found solace and support in an LGBTQ+ support group, where he connected with others who had experienced similar rejections. Through shared stories and collective support, Liam learned coping mechanisms that helped him reconcile his need for familial love with the necessity of protecting his well-being. Over time, he cultivated a sense of self-love and acceptance that no external rejection could diminish.

Building supportive environments within these complex dynamics involves intentional actions and empathetic understanding. Strategies that have proven effective include open communication, setting clear boundaries, and actively engaging in educational conversations that challenge stereotypes and misconceptions. For instance, creating regular family meetings where members can express their thoughts and feelings in a safe and non-judgmental space can significantly enhance understanding and acceptance. Additionally, involving supportive family members or friends in these discussions can provide allies who can advocate for understanding and change from within the family structure.

These stories and strategies not only highlight the challenges faced by LGBTQ+ individuals in their relationships but also underscore the potential for growth, understanding, and unconditional love. As you navigate your relationships with family, partners, or chosen kin, remember the strength of open-hearted communication and the transformative power of acceptance and understanding. Embrace these lessons as tools that can help forge deeper connections and build supportive environments for yourself and everyone in your life.

Empowering Voices: LGBTQ+ Leaders and Innovators

In the LGBTQ+ community, there are many leaders whose work has paved the way for others. These individuals, whether in politics, the arts, science, or business, have turned personal challenges into significant achievements. Their stories not only highlight their success but also serve as inspiration for others, showing the importance of visibility and representation in leadership roles.

Take, for example, Dr. Vivian, a trailblazer in biotechnology and an openly transgender woman who has revolutionized medical approaches to transgender health care. Her journey to the top was fraught with societal challenges and professional setbacks due to her gender identity. However, her relentless pursuit of excellence and commitment to her true self broke barriers in her field. It paved the way for more inclusive practices in medical research and healthcare provision. Dr. Vivian's leadership is characterized by her innovative approach to transgender health issues, significantly improving the quality of care and support available to transgender individuals. Her visibility and success have inspired countless others in the scientific community to pursue their careers openly and authentically, reinforcing that one's gender identity is an asset, not a limitation.

In the tech world, consider Michael, a gay entrepreneur who founded a startup that develops software to improve accessibility for people with disabilities. His work addresses important needs and showcases his dedication to inclusivity and innovation. Michael's journey to success was layered with the challenge of navigating a predominantly straight, cisgender industry where LGBTQ+ individuals often face covert discrimination. However, his determination to create an inclusive company culture has set a new standard within the tech community. His company champions diversity in its hiring practices and actively participates in LGBTQ+ advocacy, leveraging its platform to push for broader societal changes. Michael's leadership exemplifies how business can be a force for social good, and his work empowers others within the community to harness their identities and drive change.

Artistically, Olivia, a non-binary artist and filmmaker, uses their platform to explore and express the nuances of queer identity. Through their highly acclaimed documentaries and art installations, Olivia challenges conventional narratives about gender and sexuality, offering new perspectives that provoke thought and foster understanding. Their journey to recognition involved many personal and professional challenges, often with traditional galleries and film festivals hesitant to accept queer-themed works. Yet, Olivia's persistence and unique artistic voice have not only garnered critical acclaim but also opened doors for other queer artists. Their leadership in the arts underscores the importance of representation, showing that authenticity in one's identity and work can break down barriers and inspire a broader acceptance and appreciation of queer experiences.

These leaders also offer invaluable advice to those aspiring to make their mark in various fields. They emphasize the importance of resilience, authenticity, and pursuing one's passions despite societal challenges. Dr. Vivian advises young LGBTQ+ individuals in science and medicine to seek mentors who can provide guidance and support, underscoring the importance of building networks that uplift and advocate for one another. Michael stresses the value of creating spaces where diversity is celebrated and actively promoted, encouraging future entrepreneurs to embed inclusivity into the core values of their business models. Meanwhile, Olivia highlights the power of storytelling and artistic expression as tools for change, urging upcoming artists to use their crafts to challenge stereotypes and advocate for social justice.

These narratives of LGBTQ+ leaders and innovators are not just inspirational but transformational. They serve as potent reminders of individuals' impact when they lead authentically and commit to inclusivity. As you reflect on these stories, consider how your experiences and identities might shape your path to leadership. Whether navigating the early stages of your career, advocating for change in your community, or simply seeking ways to make a difference, remember that your voice and actions can contribute to a legacy of empowerment and visibility for the LGBTQ+ community. Through leadership that celebrates diversity and champions inclusivity, you, too, can inspire and empower others, continuing the vital work of those who have paved the way for a more just and equitable society.

Building a Future: Hopes and Aspirations of LGBTQ+ Youth

The voices of LGBTQ+ youth are not just echoes of today; they are the clarion calls for tomorrow, painting visions of a world rich with possibilities and stripped of prejudices. These young individuals carry the dreams of personal achievement and the collective hope for a community that thrives on equality and acceptance. Their aspirations, from becoming leaders and innovators to simply living authentically, reflect personal ambitions and a deeper desire to shape a society that embraces all identities with openness and respect.

Consider the aspirations of Terry, a young transgender teen aspiring to become a human rights lawyer. Terry dreams of a future where legal systems worldwide understand and protect the rights of LGBTQ+ individuals without hesitation or prejudice. The barriers, however, are substantial—from educational environments that still grapple with inclusivity to societal norms that often stigmatize trans identities. Yet, Terry's plan to overcome these obstacles is rooted in education and advocacy. By pursuing a degree in law and volunteering with LGBTQ+ advocacy groups, Terry aims to equip themselves with the knowledge and skills needed to effect change both in the courtroom and beyond. Terry's story is a testament to the power of youthful optimism and the impact that one determined individual can have on the broader fight for equality.

Then there's Lane, who dreams of starting a nonprofit that supports homeless LGBTQ+ youth. Lane's vision stems from their own experiences of instability and the lack of adequate support systems that cater specifically to the unique needs of LGBTQ+ young people. The barriers are daunting: funding, public awareness, and systemic indifference. Yet, Lane is still determined and planning to study social work and nonprofit management. By building a network of mentors and allies and harnessing the power of social media to raise awareness, Lane is laying the groundwork for a future where no LGBTQ+ youth must face homelessness alone.

These stories underscore the crucial role of supportive systems —mentors, educational opportunities, and community networks—in helping LGBTQ+ youth realize their dreams. Mentorship, in particular, plays a pivotal role. Mentors provide guidance, encouragement, and the wisdom of experience, helping young individuals navigate the complexities of their personal and professional lives. Educational programs focusing on LGBTQ+ issues, leadership development, and career readiness further equip these young minds with the tools they need to succeed and lead.

The aspirations of LGBTQ+ youth do more than just outline hopes for personal success; they sketch a blueprint for the ongoing fight for equality and acceptance. Each dream adds a layer to the foundation of a more inclusive society, and each achievement is a step towards a future where being LGBTQ+ is no longer a barrier to safety, success, or happiness. By supporting these young voices, nurturing their dreams, and breaking down the barriers they face, we contribute to a richer world in achievements, compassion, and understanding.

As we close this chapter, we carry forward not just the stories of challenges and triumphs but a renewed commitment to support the aspirations of LGBTQ+ youth. Their dreams, vibrant and varied, are reminders of the work that still lies ahead and the potential that future generations hold. Let us resolve to listen, support, and advocate for these young voices, ensuring that their dreams are not deferred but realized in all their brilliant colors.

Conclusion

As we draw the curtains on this journey through the pages of the *LGBTQ+ Mental Health and Advocacy Guide*, I am filled with immense gratitude and a renewed sense of purpose. We've explored resilience, diversity, and empowerment, highlighting the varied experiences within the LGBTQ+ community. You've seen firsthand the strength that pulses through every story of adversity and every tale of triumph.

Reflecting on our journey, it's clear that understanding LGBTQ+ identities and experiences is not just about acknowledging these identities but also about appreciating how they intersect with other aspects of life—race, disability, socioeconomic status, and more. These intersections aren't just footnotes; they are central to the narrative of each individual, shaping the unique challenges and remarkable resilience that define the community.

We've delved deep into mental health strategies tailored to the LGBTQ+ community. From evidence-based interventions to the critical necessity of gender-affirming care and robust suicide prevention measures, the importance of specialized support cannot be overstated. Mental health is a pivotal battleground in the fight for equality, and equipped with the right tools and understanding, we can make significant strides in safeguarding our community's well-being.

Navigating family and societal interactions often requires a blend of grace and resilience. This book offers strategies for handling rejection, building chosen families, and fostering supportive networks that uphold and celebrate LGBTQ+ identities. These tools are vital for surviving and thriving in environments that may not always understand or accept us.

Advocacy and legal rights have been a cornerstone of our discussions. Understanding your rights, engaging in grassroots advocacy, and pushing for inclusive policies in educational and workplace environments are more than actions—they are the framework for sustained change. Each step you take builds on the legacy of those who marched before us, paving the way for a more just and equitable society.

In addressing healthcare and wellness, we underscored the urgent need for LGBTQ+ affirming providers and competent mental health care. The holistic approaches to well-being detailed here are not just recommendations; they are essential strategies catering to our community's unique needs, ensuring everyone has access to the care and support they deserve.

Our exploration of educational and workplace inclusion highlighted the transformative power of developing LGBTQ+ inclusive curricula, establishing safe spaces, and enacting inclusive workplace policies. These initiatives are about creating less hostile environments and fostering spaces that celebrate and amplify diversity.

The wealth of community support and resources available—from online platforms and local organizations to hotlines and community centers—illustrates a vibrant aid network ready to be tapped into. These resources are lifelines, essential for those seeking support, guidance, or a sense of belonging.

The personal narratives shared have enriched this book and demonstrated the profound impact of storytelling. These stories foster empathy, understanding, and empowerment, bridging divides and knitting us closer as a community. They remind us that behind every statistic and every headline are individuals with hopes, fears, and dreams.

While we have made remarkable progress, the journey towards full equality and acceptance continues. I urge you, dear reader, not just to apply the insights from this book in your own life but to step up as an advocate for change. Whether by supporting a friend, participating in community events, or leading an advocacy campaign, your actions create ripples that expand outward.

As we part ways on this written journey, I invite you to carry the torch of education and engagement. Dive into further reading, get involved with advocacy groups, and continue participating in community events. Your journey of learning and advocacy is far from over—it's just beginning.

Thank you for your openness to learning, growing, and contributing to the dialogue surrounding LGBTQ+ rights and mental health. Remember, each of us, regardless of where we stand on the LGBTQ+ spectrum or our role as allies, holds the power to contribute to a more inclusive, understanding, and compassionate world. With hope and solidarity, let's continue our shared mission toward a future where everyone can be themselves.

Together, we are unstoppable.

Now that you have everything you need to support mental health and advocate for LGBTQ+ rights, it's time to share your newfound knowledge and show other readers where they can find the same support.

Leaving your honest opinion of this book on Amazon will help other LGBTQ+ individuals and allies find the guidance they need to navigate their journey with confidence and pride.

Scan the QR code to leave your review on Amazon.

Let's keep pride alive, pass on the torch of knowledge, and support future LGBTQ+ advocates. Your role in this journey is crucial, and I am profoundly grateful for your help in making LGBTQ+ mental health and advocacy more accessible and celebrated.

Here's to continuing our journey with new knowledge and a shared purpose. Thank you for being an essential part of this adventure.

Your biggest fan,

Alex Harper

References

- *Understanding the Gender Identity Spectrum* https://www.family-institute.org/behavioral-health-resources/understanding-gender-identity-spectrum
- *Kimberlé Crenshaw on Intersectionality, More than Two Decades Later* https://www.law.columbia.edu/news/archive/kimberle-crenshaw-intersectionality-more-two-decades-later
- *LGBTQ+ Communities and Mental Health* https://www.mhanational.org/issues/lgbtq-communities-and-mental-health
- *LGBTQ Rights Timeline in American History* https://lgbtqhistory.org/lgbt-rights-timeline-in-american-history/
- *2023 U.S. National Survey on the Mental Health of LGBTQ …* https://www.thetrevorproject.org/survey-2023/
- *Understanding LGBTQ-Affirmative Psychotherapy* https://psychcentral.com/blog/sex/2014/04/understanding-lgbtq-affirmative-psychotherapy
- *Gender dysphoria - Diagnosis and treatment* https://www.mayoclinic.org/diseases-conditions/gender-dysphoria/diagnosis-treatment/drc-20475262
- *Preventing suicide in LGBTQ communities* https://afsp.org/preventing-suicide-in-lgbtq-communities/
- *The Coming Out Handbook* https://www.thetrevorproject.org/resources/guide/the-coming-out-handbook/
- *Family Rejection as a Predictor of Negative Health …* https://publications.aap.org/pediatrics/article/123/1/346/71912/Family-Rejection-as-a-Predictor-of-Negative-Health
- *A Christian Conversation Guide* https://www.hrc.org/resources/a-christian-conversation-guide
- *Know Your Rights | LGBTQ Rights | ACLU* https://www.aclu.org/know-your-rights/lgbtq-rights
- *List of LGBT-related cases in the United States Supreme Court* https://en.wikipedia.org/wiki/List_of_LGBT-related_cases_in_the_United_States_Supreme_Court
- *Six steps to effective LGBT human rights advocacy* https://www.ilga-

europe.org/files/uploads/2022/04/Make-It-Work-Six-steps-effective-LGBT-human-rights-advocacy.pdf

- *DEVELOPING LGBTQ-INCLUSIVE CLASSROOM ...* https://www.glsen.org/sites/default/files/2019-11/GLSEN_LGBTQ_Inclusive_Curriculum_Resource_2019_0.pdf
- *Protections Against Employment Discrimination Based on ...* https://www.eeoc.gov/laws/guidance/protections-against-employment-discrimination-based-sexual-orientation-or-gender
- *OutCare Health - LGBTQ+ Healthcare Resources & Providers* https://www.outcarehealth.org/
- *Overview of gender-affirming treatments and procedures* https://transcare.ucsf.edu/guidelines/overview
- *Health Coverage Guide* https://transequality.org/health-coverage-guide
- *How to Contribute to the Holistic Wellness of the LGBTQIA+ ...* https://www.integrativenutrition.com/blog/how-to-help-lgbtqia-organizations
- *LGBTQ-Inclusive Curriculum as a Path to Better Public Health* https://www.americanbar.org/groups/crsj/publications/human_rights_magazine_home/intersection-of-lgbtq-rights-and-religious-freedom/lgbtq-inclusive-curriculum-as-a-path-to-better-public-health/
- *Safe Schools Program for LGBTQ students* https://www.mass.gov/info-details/safe-schools-program-for-lgbtq-students
- *Ensuring Workplace Inclusion for LGBTQ+ Employees* https://www.shrm.org/topics-tools/tools/toolkits/ensuring-workplace-inclusion-lgbtq--employees
- *Creating a Trans-Inclusive Workplace* https://hbr.org/2020/03/creating-a-trans-inclusive-workplace
- *The Trevor Project - Suicide Prevention for LGBTQ+ Young ...* https://www.thetrevorproject.org/
- *Human Rights Campaign* https://www.hrc.org/
- *LGBTQ+ Communities and Mental Health* https://www.mhanational.org/issues/lgbtq-communities-and-mental-health
- *How to Make Virtual Conferences Queer-Friendly: A Guide* https://www.queerinai.com/how-to-make-virtual-conferences-queer-friendly
- *2023 U.S. National Survey on the Mental Health of LGBTQ ...* https://www.thetrevorproject.org/survey-2023/

- *Courage and sacrifice: 6 activists behind LGBTQ progress* https://www.cnn.com/2019/06/26/us/most-influential-lgbtq-activists/index.html
- *What Do I Need to Know About the Transitioning Process?* https://www.plannedparenthood.org/learn/gender-identity/transgender/what-do-i-need-know-about-transitioning
- *LGBT Youth and Family Acceptance - PMC - NCBI* https://www.ncbi.nlm.nih.gov/pmc/articles/PMC5127283/

www.ingramcontent.com/pod-product-compliance
Lightning Source LLC
Chambersburg PA
CBHW071954150726
47999CB00001B/440